The Art of Collaboration

The Art of Collaboration

*Chamber Music Rehearsal Techniques
and Team Building*

ANNIE FULLARD
AND
DORIANNE COTTER-LOCKARD

Oxford University Press is a department of the University of Oxford.
It furthers the University's objective of excellence in research, scholarship,
and education by publishing worldwide. Oxford is a registered trade mark of
Oxford University Press in the UK and certain other countries.

Published in the United States of America by Oxford University Press
198 Madison Avenue, New York, NY 10016, United States of America.

© Oxford University Press 2025

All rights reserved. No part of this publication may be reproduced, stored in a retrieval system, transmitted, used for text and data mining, or used for training artificial intelligence, in any form or by any means, without the prior permission in writing of Oxford University Press, or as expressly permitted by law, by license or under terms agreed with the appropriate reprographics rights organization. Inquiries concerning reproduction outside the scope of the above should be sent to the Rights Department, Oxford University Press, at the address above.

You must not circulate this work in any other form
and you must impose this same condition on any acquirer

Library of Congress Cataloging-in-Publication Data
Names: Fullard, Annie, 1963– author. | Cotter-Lockard, Dorianne, author.
Title: The art of collaboration : chamber music rehearsal techniques and
teambuilding / Annie Fullard & Dorianne Cotter-Lockard.
Description: New York : Oxford University Press, 2025. |
Includes bibliographical references and index.
Identifiers: LCCN 2024038466 (print) | LCCN 2024038467 (ebook) |
ISBN 9780197673133 (paperback) | ISBN 9780197673126 (hardback) |
ISBN 9780197673157 (epub)
Subjects: LCSH: Chamber music—Instruction and study. | Music rehearsals.
Classification: LCC MT728 .F85 2025 (print) | LCC MT728 (ebook) |
DDC 785.044—dc23/eng/20240909
LC record available at https://lccn.loc.gov/2024038466
LC ebook record available at https://lccn.loc.gov/2024038467

DOI: 10.1093/oso/9780197673126.001.0001

Paperback printed by Integrated Books International, United States of America
Hardback printed by Bridgeport National Bindery, Inc., United States of America

The manufacturer's authorised representative in the EU for product safety is Oxford University Press España S.A. of El Parque Empresarial San Fernando de Henares, Avenida de Castilla, 2 – 28830 Madrid (www.oup.es/en or product.safety@oup.com). OUP España S.A. also acts as importer into Spain of products made by the manufacturer.

We dedicate this book to everyone who shares a love of chamber music.

Contents

Foreword—by Peter Salaff xiii
Preface xv
Acknowledgments xix
How to Use This Book as a Resource xxi
About the Companion Website xxiii

Introduction 1
- Our Mission 1
- Why This Book? 1
- Who Is This Book For? 2
- Who We Are 2
- Our Vision 4
- Triad of Chamber Music Roles 4
- Voices of Our Teachers and Mentors 5
- Voices of Our Colleagues and Former Students 5
- How This Book Is Organized 6
  - Part I: Collaboration Basics to Build Your Team 6
  - Part II: Rehearsal Preparation and Process 6
  - Part III: Inspiration and Interpretation 6
  - Part IV: Techniques for Productive Rehearsals 7
- Key Concepts in This Book 7

PART I COLLABORATION BASICS TO BUILD YOUR TEAM

1 Our Rehearsal and Teaching Philosophy 11
- Working with Love and Inspiration 11
  - Love 11
  - Inspiration 12
- The Importance of Relationships 13
- Creating a Positive Environment 14
  - Respectful Communication 15
  - Empathy 15
  - Playfulness, Joy, and Laughter 16
  - Co-Leadership 17

2 Working Well Together 18
- Foundations to Build the Collaborative Team and Create a Positive Environment 18
  - Appreciation 19
  - Inquiry and Invitation 20
  - Listening 20
  - Energy 21
  - Collaborative Dialogue 22
- Causes of Tension and Conflict 23
  - Blaming or Personalizing 24
  - Taking Things Personally 24

viii Contents

Lack of Focus	25
Misunderstandings and Assumptions	25
Strongly Held Views	26
Not Following Through	26
Strategies for Working Well Together	26
Try Every Idea as if It Were Your Own	27
Rule of Agreement from Comedy Theater Improv	28
Compromise Equals Improvement	29
Laugh Together, Play Together	30
Respect Personalities	31
Emotional Intelligence	32
Bring Your Best Self	33
Summary	33

PART II REHEARSAL PREPARATION AND PROCESS

3 Individual Preparation

	37
Parts and Scores	37
Acquiring Parts and Scores	38
Measure Numbers—Where Are We?	38
Practicing Your Individual Part	40
Challenging Passages	40
Repetition	41
Rhythmic Variations	41
Intonation	41
Dynamics	42
Rhythms	42
The Metronome	43
A Note Regarding Beethoven's Tempo Markings	43
Additional Helpful Hints	44
Developing Your Interpretation	45
Exploring the Score	45
Using Media as a Resource	45
An Invitation to Be Curious	46
What to Bring to Rehearsal (and Coaching Sessions)	47
Co-Leadership: Your Role in the Ensemble	47

4 Score Study

	49
Editions of Parts and Scores	49
Identifying Key Elements of the Score	50
Tempo and Character	51
Melodic Themes and Motives	52
Rhythmic Cues	53
Identify Rhythmic Partners: Buddy System	54
Circle All Silences	54
Dynamics	55
Harmony	58
Form and Structure	59
An Invitation to Play from the Score	60
Have Fun with Your Score: An Exercise	60

Contents ix

5 Rehearsal Playbook   63
　Long-Range Plan   63
　Daily Rehearsal Plan   64
　　Tuning Routine   65
　　Warmup Routine   65
　　Rehearsing Spots   65
　　Daily Rehearsal Plan Example   66
　Organizing Accountabilities   67
　Healthy Communication During Rehearsal   69
　　Using Focus Words or Phrases   69
　　Positive Communication While Rehearsing Spots   69

PART III INSPIRATION AND INTERPRETATION

6 Exploring the Character   73
　Interpreting Moods, Emotions, and Meaning   73
　　Descriptive Words   74
　　Historical References   75
　　Singing or Dancing?   76
　Finding Your Tonal Color Palette   76
　　Hear the Color (Ode to Oliver Sacks)   77
　Engaging Your Imagination   81
　Storytelling   81
　Drawing Inspiration from Around the World   83

7 Exploring the Composer's World   84
　Investigating the Era: Trends and Styles   84
　　Viewing Art and Architecture   85
　　Exploring Literature   87
　　Observing the Natural World   87
　Exploring the Composer's Voice   88
　　Researching Life Events   88
　　Listening to Other Works by the Composer   89
　　Reading Letters and Quotes   89
　Collaborating with Living Composers   91
　　Meeting the Composer: Gabriela Lena Frank   91
　　Developing a Composer's Mindset   93
　　Developing a Composer's Mindset Through Improvisation   94
　　Improvising Together: An Exercise   94

PART IV TECHNIQUES FOR PRODUCTIVE REHEARSALS

8 Techniques for Cueing and Breathing Together   99
　Sharing the Cueing Responsibility: Initiator and Inspirer   100
　Pantomime Cueing: Finding Your "Inner Conductor"   101
　Conducting and Breathing Together   102
　Cueing with Your Instruments   103
　　Using the Zone of Silence   103
　　Cueing for Wind and Brass Players   104
　　Helpful Hints on Cueing   104

x Contents

Individual Practice	105
Ensemble Practice	105
Final Hints	106

9 Techniques for Rhythmic Alignment and Ensemble — 107

Synchronizing Your Movement: *Chamber Music Aerobics*	108
Expressive Counting: *Shakespearean Counting*	109
The Metronome Is Your Friend	110
Establishing Visual Connection: Look Up Once per Measure	111
Passing the Melody or Motive	112
Synchronizing Rhythmic Subdivisions	115
Exaggerating Tempos	117
Playing in Slow Motion: *Discovery Tempo*	117
Playing at Hyper-Speed	117
Achieving a Long Line	118
Clapping Rhythms Together	118
Playing Composite Rhythms	118
Understanding Syncopation	120
Left Hands Alone "à la Sasha Schneider"	121
Creating Rubato Through Agogic Playing	123

10 Techniques for Intonation — 124

Intonation Approach	124
Tuning Routine	125
Tuning for String Ensembles	125
Vertical Listening	126
Melodic and Vertical Intonation	127
Warmup Routine with Intonation Techniques	128
Playing Scales	128
Variations	129
Playing Bach Chorales	129
Four-Tone Tuning Exercise	130
Tuning Passages from Repertoire	130
Understanding Musical Texture	131
General Steps for Tuning Passages	131
Unison or Octave (Monophonic) Passages	131
Chordal (Homophonic) Passages	132
A Listening Exercise: Tuning to a Drone	133
Tuning as a Meditation	133

11 Techniques for Sound Production — 135

Achieving a Blended and Resonant Sound	135
Vocal Inspiration: Name That Singer	136
Apply Vocal Technique Concepts	136
Articulation and Diction	137
Staccato: Dots and Wedges	137
Legato: Slurs and Phrase Markings	139
Emphasis Markings—Sforzando, Fortepiano, Tenuto	140
Sforzando (sfz)	140

Contents   xi

Fortepiano (*fp*) 141
Tenuto (𝄐) 142
Articulations—General Guidance 142
Vibrato: To Vibrate or Not to Vibrate 142
String Instrument Techniques for Sound Production 143
The Bow 143
Vibrato Technique 144
Kinesthetic Sound Production Techniques 144
Kinesthetic Approach—Connect Right and Left Hands 145
Focus the Sound: Playing Ponticello 145
Woodwind and Brass Techniques for Sound Production 146
Piano Techniques for Sound Production 147
Listening, Balance, and Sound Palette 148
Piano Techniques for Controlling Dynamics 148
Touch and Response 150

12 Techniques for Projecting Expression 151
Singing 151
Chamber Works Inspired by Song 152
Scat Singing 153
Standing 155
Stand and Play 155
Stand and Walk 156
Expressing Dynamics 157
Practicing Dynamics Together 157
Playing the Silences 158
Creating Your Dynamic Chart 158
Playing to the Center 160
Playing by Memory 160

13 Techniques for Strategic Listening and Balance 162
Shining the Light 162
The Listening Game 164
Switching Seats 164
Playing with Backs to Each Other 165

14 The Capstone Technique: Live, Breathe, and Die (LBAD) 167
Theater Mirroring Exercise 167
LBAD 169

Appendix A: Resources 173
Appendix B: Descriptive Words 179
Appendix C: Rehearsal Plan Summary 183
Appendix D: Sound Production Techniques for Strings: The Bow 185
Appendix E: Contributors to the Book 189
Notes 191
Bibliography 197

Foreword—by Peter Salaff

I have known the Cavani Quartet since 1985 when they were chosen as winners of The Cleveland Quartet Competition at the Eastman School of Music. My colleagues and I were very impressed with the Cavani Quartet's very special sound and their deeply communicative, energetic, and imaginative playing. They have a natural empathy and profound respect for the music. They share ideas with one another, and the audience, with compelling grace and love.

As their coaches, my colleagues and I passed on ideas of quartet playing to the Cavani Quartet that we learned from the immortal members of the Budapest, Juilliard, and New Music Quartets. Today, the Cavani Quartet continues this very special legacy, developing the ideas that they learned from the Cleveland, Juilliard, and Tokyo Quartets. This legacy continues to connect us all, as the Cavani Quartet serves as a mentor for groups who are successfully pursuing careers in music. Through their teaching, they constantly strive to help everyone to find their inner artist, and to realize their own unique, special potential.

I feel privileged and honored to have worked with the Cavani String Quartet at The Cleveland Institute of Music. It was really a wonderful collaboration based on great admiration and respect for one another. It is certainly one of the highlights of my life. The members of the quartet are all exceptional, caring human beings who are devoted to helping their students to play at their highest artistic level. They continually encourage their students to inspire and support each other.

The Cavani Quartet members teach with great knowledge, passion, energy, and joy. I have learned so much from their incredibly imaginative and creative ideas, and I am glad to be a part of a book that brings these rehearsal techniques to life in order to share them with a larger audience. It has been wonderful to get to know Dorianne while she was conducting her doctoral research at the Cleveland Institute of Music. I was happy to participate in the seminars and coaching sessions that she recorded, as well as engage in dialogue with her about the rehearsal techniques and the chamber music coaching process.

This book is a wonderful guide which will be helpful for the next generation of musicians. The perspective of this book also serves as a larger message for the world, which is that music connects us in a beautiful way as human beings.

Peter Salaff
Founding member, Cleveland String Quartet
Former Professor of Violin at the Eastman School of Music
Former Director of String Chamber Music at the Cleveland Institute of Music

Preface

We first met face-to-face on a sunny spring day in a coffee shop in Berkeley, California. We fell into an animated conversation about chamber music and how important it was in our lives and immediately felt a kinship that ignited our passion to collaborate on a project. Prior to our first meeting, Dorianne sent inquiries to several string quartets and music scholars while conducting initial research for her dissertation. Annie responded with a two-page list of specific Cavani Quartet rehearsal techniques and coaching strategies, and an invitation to "come visit us—there is an entire chamber music education 'laboratory' going on here at the Cleveland Institute of Music—and it would be fun to share it with you!!" A month later, Dorianne came to hear the Cavani Quartet perform while on tour in California, meeting Annie for coffee and entering a collaboration that has continued beyond the initial research project.

Dorianne: I grew up with a strong education in chamber music and subsequently attended the Eastman School of Music for my undergraduate degree. I learned early on how the language of chamber music could bring together people from different corners of the earth to play music in harmony and synchrony, despite cultural differences and language barriers. After a few years as a professional musician, I changed direction and spent the next twenty-five years in the corporate work world as a leader of technology organizations and a consultant to the Fortune 500. Seeking a new direction in my work, I left my role as a leader of organizations in 2007 to enter a doctoral program in human and organizational development, deciding to conduct research on how teams learn to collaborate. I returned to my roots by using the example of a string quartet to illustrate how team collaboration can work.

Annie: The Cavani Quartet has been an integral part of my life since we formed in 1984 when I was a sophomore in college. The study and performance of chamber music with mentors and colleagues continues to ignite and inspire me as an artist and human being. By the time I met Dorianne, I had documented a list of Cavani Quartet rehearsal techniques and coaching strategies for a chamber music pedagogy course at the Cleveland Institute of Music (CIM). Our training and mentorship with the members of the Cleveland, Juilliard, and Tokyo string quartets, along with other formative chamber music coaches, are reflected in these techniques. We established a unique team-teaching approach with Peter Salaff at CIM, exchanging ideas and offering students techniques to help them with the rehearsal process to achieve extraordinary, empathetic musical experiences. Dorianne's inquiry highlighted the deeper message of chamber music playing as a collaborative, human endeavor. Our aim as artist-teachers is to help ensembles connect with—and bring out the best in— each other to communicate more expressively to their audience. We find that this approach inspires the highest level of performance. As I started working with Dorianne on this research project, my colleagues and I came to articulate more clearly our goal for our program: To help students develop musical leadership in which they have an equal voice in the ensemble, applying the most positive attributes of the human spirit, such as kindness and generosity, into the rehearsal process.

Dorianne: My dissertation study documented how the Cavani Quartet used their coaching strategies and rehearsal techniques to teach students to work effectively as teams. A *coaching strategy* is a combination of the coaching style, rehearsal techniques, and areas of emphasis used by the coaches to guide their students during a coaching session. A *rehearsal technique* is a specific practice taught by the coaches in coaching sessions and used by students during their rehearsals. I documented the set of techniques in my dissertation, organizing the elements of the Cavani Quartet's coaching process.

My primary goal in conducting this research was to gain a deeper understanding of the Cavani Quartet's process of coaching string quartets. My secondary goal was to gain an understanding of how the coaching process helped string quartets learn to collaborate effectively. In addition, I endeavored to draw connections between the chamber music coaching process and ways in which organizational teams can learn to work together.

Annie: We founded our quartet in 1984 (Annie Fullard, violin; Susan Waterbury, violin; Erika Eckert, viola; Merry Peckham, cello), and in 1988 we were invited by CIM president David Cerone to join the faculty as the resident string quartet. Over the course of the past forty years, the quartet has led a robust performing, touring, and teaching life. In 1993 and 1995, respectively, Mari Sato (violin) and Kirsten Docter (viola) joined the quartet. Eric Wong (viola) joined the quartet in the fall of 2015. Kyle Price (cello) and Catherine Cosbey (violin) joined the quartet in 2019. For the past two seasons, Ayane Kozasa and Samuel Rosenthal have served as guest violists.

Along the way, we have been nationally recognized for programs developed to serve student ensembles devoted to the serious study of chamber music. These include *The Intensive Quartet Seminar, The Apprentice Quartet Program, The Art of Collaboration: Rehearsal Techniques Seminar*, and *The Art of Engagement: Careers and Leadership in Music*. In addition, three decades ago, we created a program called *Team Up with Music*, devoted to school-aged children. The objective was to ignite their interest in stringed instruments and chamber music. Dorianne and I concluded that the work of the Cavani Quartet would support the vision of her research topic.

Dorianne: As I learned more about the work of the Cavani Quartet and the programs they created and led; it became clear that their work aligned with my research interests; namely, how people learn to collaborate effectively. The analogy of the string quartet as a small, self-managing team resonated perfectly with my desire to draw connections between the world of organizations and the world of chamber musicians. And, by wonderful coincidence, we studied with many of the same teachers such as the Cleveland and Tokyo string quartets. For me, it was gratifying to step back into the music conservatory environment to conduct my research. Since then, my collaborations with Cavani Quartet, Peter Salaff, and Annie have evolved into treasured long-term friendships.

We believe that the art of collaboration in chamber music encompasses more than the craft of playing one's instrument well. A small group of people, through a creative alliance, can inspire a larger worldview that honors humanity, the expression of diverse perspectives, and the generation of love through music.

Annie Fullard
Dorianne Cotter-Lockard
August 31, 2024

Acknowledgments

We owe a huge debt of gratitude to our families who supported, encouraged, and lovingly cajoled us to finish the book: our partners "The Jims" Jim Rosenthal and Jim Lockard as well as our brilliant children Grace Stauffer, Heather Lockard, Samuel Rosenthal, and Haruno Sato. Annie is especially grateful to her parents, Marcia Ferritto and William Fullard, and her extended family, Mim, Mel, Jeanne, and Ann Rosenthal for their unconditional love. Dorianne acknowledges and celebrates the musical spirit of her father, Stan Cotter, and his wife, Corienne, for their love and support. Annie also wishes to extend her gratitude to Ronald and Betty Crutcher for their unflagging encouragement and love.

There would be no book without the contributions and love provided by all the members of the Cavani Quartet, former and current. We acknowledge Erika Eckert, Kirsten Docter, Merry Peckham, Mari Sato, Susan Waterbury, and Eric Wong, as well as Catherine Cosbey, Kyle Price, and Ayane Kozasa for being extraordinary colleagues.

There are not enough words to properly acknowledge the contribution Peter Salaff made to the mission of writing this book and his impact on the Cavani Quartet. Peter's encouragement influenced the book throughout our writing journey. From the inception of Dorianne's doctoral research to writing the foreword to reviewing the entire manuscript prior to production, he has inspired us and modeled what it means to collaborate successfully.

We also wish to acknowledge and thank the other members of the Cleveland Quartet, including James Dunham, Paul Katz, Martha Strongin Katz, and Donald Weilerstein, for their contributions and for helping us to celebrate their tremendous legacy as our teachers and mentors. We are especially grateful to former members of the Juilliard String Quartet, Earl Carlyss and Joel Krosnick, who provided wisdom and insights through our interviews with them. In addition, we are thankful to be able to draw upon the memory of our work with the late Robert Mann, one of the most influential chamber musicians of the twentieth century.

We are grateful to early reviewers of our book proposal, Don Rosenberg, Hartmut Kuhlmann, John Byrne, and Petru Dan, as well as Greg Smith for copyediting our proposal. Our book took shape through the development coaching of Jeffrey Davis at Tracking Wonder and review and editing support of Aaron Cohen at Written World Consulting. We are grateful for the continuous guidance and support of Michelle Chen and Rachel Ruisard from Oxford University Press as well as the anonymous reviewers engaged by OUP who provided feedback to aid in our book development.

We are grateful to Gabriela Lena Frank for helping us to create an informed section in our book on working with living composers. Imani Winds bassoonist Monica Ellis and former Imani member and French Hornist Jeff Scott provided insights

xx Acknowledgments

related to playing in wind ensembles. Pianists Vivian Hornik Weilerstein and Anton Nel offered wonderful ideas about the art of piano chamber music playing.

We thank all our interviewees who willingly shared their experiences as chamber musicians and whose quotes are included throughout the book, including Mike Block, Alex Cox, Ronald Crutcher, David Finkel, Norman Fischer, Elizabeth Hankins, Joseph Kromholz, Megan Frievogel McDonough, Anton Nel, Elizabeth Oakes, Peter Oundjian, Karla Donehew Perez, Deborah Price, Tom Rosenberg, Amy Schwartz-Moretti, Astrid Schween, Vivian Hornik Weilerstein, Carol Wincenc, Andrew Yee, and Hyeyung Sol Yoon.

Annie would like to especially thank the thousands of young instrumentalists whom she has been lucky enough to interact with during her years as a chamber music coach. These students make the world better and are the catalyst for this book. We also thank the amateur chamber music community in France, who welcomed Annie as coach on numerous occasions while we worked on the book and who continue to learn and perform chamber music with Dorianne.

Dorianne is eternally grateful for the teaching and mentoring of Anne Crowden, who insisted that all her violin students play chamber music as an essential part of their musical development. Dorianne would also like to thank her dissertation committee, who supported the research which eventually led to this book: Valerie Bentz, David Rehorick, Jeremy Shapiro, and external reviewer Elaine King.

Finally, Dorianne and Annie would like to thank their cats, Simone, Art, and Mewzik for years of standing on their computers while we tried to work and for frequent snuggles.

Further acknowledgments:

Bach 24 Chorales reharmonized (Chorale no. 20, BWV 302, measures 1–4) by David Bynog. Open-source permission via Journal of the American Viola Society.

String Quartet No. 4, SZ91 by Béla Bartók (measures 1–15), © Copyright 1929 by Boosey & Hawkes. Reproduced by permission of Boosey & Hawkes.

Quartet Op. 1, No. 4, Rondeau by Joseph Bologne, Chevalier de St. George. Score realized from parts by David Wolfson, with permission from David Wolfson.

Leyendas: An Andean Walkabout (VI. Coqueteos, measures 1–31) by Gabriela Lena Frank, Copyright © 2003 by G. Schirmer, Inc. International Copyright Secured. All Rights Reserved. Used with permission.

How to Use This Book as a Resource

This book is organized so you can easily find sections that address the challenges you seek to explore and resolve. While some may want to read in the order presented, others may choose to jump to parts based on the needs of their ensemble.

The appendices include a list of resources, a bibliography, and supplemental materials related to the techniques. In addition, you can find video clips of many of the techniques on our website: The Art of Collaboration (https://www.chambermusiccollaboration.com).

Use this book the way you might treat yourself to your favorite chocolate bar. Most of us love to break off a small piece at a time and savor the experience which offers a joyful moment of contemplation or a kick of energy when you most need it. A great chocolate bar should be shared so everyone enjoys a taste! Cavani violinist, Catherine Cosbey loves to have a chocolate bar on hand for a shared healthy snack during our rehearsals. In the same way, this book should be used in small "bites" as a resource with instant access to solutions for rehearsal challenges.

Using the table of contents as your guide, note that the book is divided into four large sections (Parts I–IV), each includes specific topics with instructions and strategies related to the rehearsal process.

Following is a quick guide to *The Art of Collaboration: Chamber Music Rehearsal Techniques and Team Building*.

Need help getting along and working together? See Part I, Chapters 1–2

Develop a value system for respectful, productive rehearsals within your ensemble, based on heathy relationships and conflict resolution techniques.

Need help preparing for rehearsals? See Part II, Chapters 3–4

Organize your approach to individual preparation, which includes score study and strategies for practicing your part.

Need to have a more organized and efficient rehearsal? See Part II, Chapter 5

Improve your rehearsal productivity by organizing and structuring your time.

Need more inspiration for group interpretation? See Part III, Chapter 6

Illuminate ways to ignite your interpretive process. This chapter offers approaches for developing your interpretive palette through descriptive words, visual art, dance, storytelling, and exploring music from around the world.

Need help researching the composer? See Part III, Chapter 7

Deepen your understanding of the composer's life and times through exploration and research. This chapter includes a section devoted to working with living composers.

Need a technique to solve a problem that arises during your rehearsal? See Part IV, Chapters 8–14

Cueing? See Chapter 8
Rhythm? See Chapter 9
Intonation? See Chapter 10
Sound production? See Chapter 11
Projection and expression? See Chapter 12
Listening? Chapter 13
Connection and Communication? See Chapter 14

About the Companion Website

www.oup.com/us/TheArtofCollaboration

Oxford has created a website to accompany *The Art of Collaboration: Chamber Music Rehearsal Techniques and Teambuilding*. Material that cannot be made available in a book, namely video demonstrations of selected techniques, is provided here. The reader is encouraged to consult this resource in conjunction with the chapters.

INTRODUCTION

Our Mission

The mission of this book is to promote team building and facilitate rehearsal practices that *bond*, rather than divide, an ensemble. These processes liberate ensembles to create deeper, more collaborative performances. As a result, ensembles achieve a higher level of performance. Primary to this mission is cultivating shared empathy and connection in performing and teaching chamber music, which we value as a metaphor for the type of communication we wish to see expressed around the world.

Why This Book?

Playing chamber music is a catalyst—not only for deepening the expressive power of music, but also for building a connected and synergistic ensemble.

The Art of Collaboration: Chamber Music Rehearsal Techniques and Team Building is an extensive guide of rehearsal techniques for performing musicians, music educators, students, and amateur musicians who wish to improve the quality of their rehearsals and performance. This book evolved from Dorianne Cotter-Lockard's research with the Cavani String Quartet and founding member, violinist Annie Fullard.[1]

Rather than relying on the traditional apprenticeship model of motivation through negative criticism, this book provides strategies and rehearsal techniques that facilitate conflict resolution and create transformative performances. Furthermore, promoting a philosophy of equal participation and positive reinforcement provides a forum for teamwork and joyful collaboration between ensemble members.

Prior to this book, no guidebook has been written for ensembles with techniques to resolve technical challenges (e.g., tuning, ensemble, sound, rhythmic alignment, and intonation) *and* strategies for successful collaboration. This book offers a variety of rehearsal techniques to not only improve the sound and quality of performances but also create an empathetic, safe environment for each ensemble member's voice to be heard and respected. Moreover, these methods encourage each member to take a leadership role in the group, ensuring that diverse perspectives are valued and heard.

Most of the approaches and techniques in this book can be applied to a wide range of instrumental and vocal musicians. The perspectives from a variety of performing artists are included in this book to support the application of these techniques.

The Art of Collaboration. Annie Fullard and Dorianne Cotter-Lockard, Oxford University Press. © Oxford University Press 2025.
DOI: 10.1093/oso/9780197673126.003.0001

2 The Art of Collaboration

These techniques form a teachable, proven system that empowers musicians to become independent learners and find their unique voice through a deeper connection with their fellow ensemble members.

Who Is This Book For?

This book is an invitation to anyone interested in cultivating a deeper understanding of how to work productively and joyfully within an ensemble, and to raise their performance level. Those who seek a rehearsal and performance environment where every voice is heard and where differing musical ideas coalesce will find the concepts in this book highly engaging and enlightening.

Music educators can utilize the ideas in this guidebook as a template for teaching and coaching students of all ages and levels. Collegiate-level students will find sage advice and specific techniques to develop efficient rehearsals and a higher standard of ensemble playing. Amateur musicians can experiment with suggestions and techniques to enhance the joy of chamber music making. Lastly, professional musicians will receive validation for best practices that create a positive, collaborative rehearsal process and elevate music performance.

Ensemble members from all musical genres can use the techniques in this book, with guidance on adapting them to a multitude of instrumental combinations. Therefore, this book represents the voices of chamber music artists from a variety of backgrounds and perspectives.

Students, teaching-artists, performers, and amateur musicians of all levels can leverage this book as a resource to enhance the rehearsal process, achieve efficient problem-solving, and experience the joy of true collaboration through music.

Who We Are

In writing this book, we discovered harmony and balance between our personalities and perspectives. We tell the story of our meeting and the collaboration process to write this book in the Preface.

Annie brings a passion for chamber music and expertise as a professional chamber music ensemble member and teaching-artist. Dorianne brings a passion for chamber music and research, writing, and leadership coaching expertise. Collectively, we bring humor, joy, laughter, and inspiring stories to our collaborative process.

Dorianne is a faculty member, teaching leadership and creativity at work at Saybrook University. She serves on the faculty at Munich Business School for the Conscious Business Education initiative and is a member of the Integral Scholars Consortium. Her coaching and consulting business, Collective Virtuosity, serves organizational leaders around the world. She has written books, articles, and chapters on authentic leadership, personal and small-group transformation, and collaboration within chamber music groups. She graduated from the Eastman School of Music and performed as a professional violinist for several years before moving to a career in technology leadership and academia.

Annie serves as Director of Chamber Music, Professor and Sidney M. Friedberg Chair, Peabody Conservatory, Johns Hopkins University. In addition she is a Distinguished Artist and the Charles and Mary Jean Yates Chair of Chamber Music at the Robert McDuffie Center for Strings, Mercer University, and chamber music faculty at Center Stage Strings. Formerly, she served as Visiting Artist and Coordinator of String Chamber Music at the University of Michigan, School of Music, Theater, and Dance. Annie served as Co–Program Director for the String Quartet Intensive at the Encore Chamber Music Institute. Annie has toured extensively throughout all fifty states and abroad and has served as a juror for the Fischoff National Chamber Music Competition, St. Paul String Quartet Competition, Midwest Young Artists Discover Competition, and Washington International Competition.

Founded in 1984 (see Figure I.1), the Cavani Quartet's legacy has garnered impressive recognition, including the Naumburg Chamber Music Award, Cleveland Quartet Award, ASCAP Award for Adventurous Programming, The Guarneri Quartet Award for Artistic Excellence, and prizes at Banff International and Fischoff

FIGURE I.1 Founding Members, Cavani Quartet, 1984, Merry Peckham, Erika Eckert, Susan Waterbury, Annie Fullard.

4 The Art of Collaboration

National chamber music competitions. They have received more than ten Chamber Music America Residency Partnership Grants. Former faculty at the Cleveland Institute of Music as Quartet in Residence, they developed renowned programs, such as the Intensive Quartet Seminar, the Apprentice Quartet Program, and the Art of Collaboration Seminar for the serious study of chamber music. Leaders in the field of chamber music education and advocacy, they have extensive expertise as visiting artists at universities and pre-college music programs worldwide in coaching string, wind, brass, percussion, and piano ensembles.

Our Vision

Our vision for the chamber music world includes performers, teaching-artists, amateurs, students and their families, and the greater community. In an ideal chamber music world, teaching-artists and students engage in continuous reciprocal learning. As teaching-artists, we give and receive inspiration from the energy and enthusiasm of our students.

A school community benefits when children learn to play chamber music. The result is a higher level of performance and more well-rounded and creative students. Playing chamber music impacts students' cognitive, emotional, and social skills in a way that enhances the general environment of the school. For example, research with high school students who play instrumental music in an ensemble shows that these experiences enhance students' cognitive capacities, motivation to learn, executive functions, and self-efficacy regardless of gender, cultural environment, or socioeconomic status.[2]

The larger community also benefits, since small ensembles can easily travel to venues outside the concert hall, such as museums, coffee shops, hospitals, community centers, shelters, libraries, and senior living centers. By performing in the community, chamber music ensembles demonstrate how working together can create a beautiful experience for both the performer and the audience.

Triad of Chamber Music Roles

Individuals who play chamber music as part of their artistic development acquire a combination of three essential musical roles: conductor, soloist, and collaborator. Chamber musicians benefit from understanding the role of a *conductor*—to interpret and analyze the score, realize the composer's intent, and gain knowledge of all the parts of the ensemble. They become kinesthetically aware, learning to cue by physically embodying rhythm, character, and meaning.

With one person to a part, chamber musicians also assume the *soloist* role, imbuing every note with life at the highest level of artistry and technique. Most significantly, chamber musicians learn how to become *collaborators* who inspire, blend,

Introduction **5**

and connect with the other members of their ensemble. The synthesis of these three roles generates powerful performances and enables a productive and creative rehearsal environment.

Voices of Our Teachers and Mentors

One of the bonds that inspired us to create this book was our shared experience of working with some of the most eminent chamber music players of our time. Our mentors and teachers modeled a legacy of remarkable spirit and collaboration during performances. Humor and vitality were always present in their teaching approach. Their generosity in sharing their knowledge inspires us as we work with our colleagues and students.

This powerful legacy is passed on to future generations of musicians by including the voices from interviews with our teachers and mentors. The Cleveland Quartet members were inspirational teachers while we studied at the Eastman School of Music. Peter Salaff, former violinist in the quartet, was the Cavani Quartet's colleague and mentor for many years at the Cleveland Institute of Music. He wrote the Foreword of this book, and we include his wisdom throughout.

Former and current members of the Cleveland, Concord, Emerson, Juilliard, and Tokyo string quartets were interviewed for the book. In addition, we include stories based on our memories of coaching sessions with the late Robert Mann, founding member of the Juilliard Quartet.

You are encouraged to honor your mentors and teachers and discover their musical legacy. After discovering a rich lineage of performance and teaching wisdom from our interviews, we believe you will feel inspired to learn who influenced and inspired your teachers.

Voices of Our Colleagues and Former Students

We are fortunate to live in an era in which there is an abundance of brilliant chamber music ensembles. We focused on interviewing those musicians who represent a variety of viewpoints and who share a common philosophy of chamber music playing.

This book would not be possible without the contributions of former and current Cavani Quartet members: Catherine Cosbey, violin; Kirsten Docter, viola; Erika Eckert, viola; Merry Peckham, cello; Ayane Kozasa, viola; Kyle Price, cello; Samuel Rosenthal, viola; Mari Sato, violin; Susan Waterbury, violin; and Eric Wong, viola.

Also included are contributions by members and former members of Aizuri Quartet, Attacca Quartet, Blair Quartet, Catalyst Quartet, Chester Quartet, Chiara Quartet, Del Sol Quartet, Ehnes Quartet, Imani Winds, Maia Quartet, Jupiter Quartet, Kronos Quartet, New York Woodwind Quintet, Omer Quartet, Silk Road Ensemble, and Thalea Quartet. Representing the voices of pianists are Anton Nel

6   The Art of Collaboration

and Vivian Weilerstein. Wisdom and guidance are provided by composer-colleague Gabriela Lena Frank on working with living composers.

We include voices of educators and artistic directors, such as Ronald Crutcher, cellist, President Emeritus, University of Richmond and Wheaton College; Tom Rosenberg, cellist, Artistic Director, Fischoff National Chamber Music Competition; Elizabeth Oakes, violist and Director, University of Iowa String Quartet Program; and Deborah Price, violist and Director, Chamber Music Connection.

How This Book Is Organized

This book is organized into four parts, each progressing from one set of concepts to the next. As you become familiar with each, you can easily navigate to the chapters that best illuminate solutions for specific challenges.

Part I: Collaboration Basics to Build Your Team

Part I offers building blocks for foundational group interaction and performance. This part begins by explaining our rehearsal and teaching philosophy that illuminates the strategies and techniques. The opening chapters address the principles and the "how to" of verbal communication within an ensemble to help each member have an equal voice. In addition, causes of tension and conflict within groups are identified, and collaboration strategies are provided. This part concludes by introducing two fundamental ideas for productive rehearsals—the comedy improvisation practice of "Yes, and . . ." and *Try Every Idea as if It Were Your Own*, moving beyond compromise toward collaboration.

Part II: Rehearsal Preparation and Process

Part II details productive rehearsal approaches, including individual preparation and score study. These chapters also provide wisdom and guidance from our mentors about pacing and organizing rehearsals.

Part III: Inspiration and Interpretation

Part III provides approaches to discovering and exploring musical language and finding inspiration by defining character, moods, emotions, and meaning. These chapters include guidance on researching the context in which composers created their works, including a section on collaboration with living composers.

Part IV: Techniques for Productive Rehearsals

Part IV details techniques to help musicians in all aspects of chamber music rehearsal and performance. Each chapter is organized by the intended purpose of the techniques, including cueing and breathing, rhythmic alignment and ensemble, intonation, sound production, projecting expression, strategic listening, and balance. The final chapter concludes with our capstone technique: *LBAD* (Live, Breathe, and Die).

Key Concepts in This Book

Listening—Cultivating deep, proactive listening is necessary to collaborate and create magical performances.

Awareness—Using all senses while playing and rehearsing. Awareness increases the ability to respond to your fellow musicians and make better use of instrumental techniques.

Empathy—Communicating with care, showing respect, and expressing kindness. Empathy extends to understanding the motivations of the composer and the emotional qualities of the music and connecting with your colleagues, the audience, and humanity.

Respect—Enabling a safe environment for the healthy exchange of ideas. Mutual respect means appreciating each other's qualities and ways of being. An environment of respect allows each person to bring their whole, authentic self to rehearsals.

Co-leadership—Instead of traditional concepts like *leading* and *following*, we use *initiating, inspiring*, and *reflecting*. Each ensemble member should assume a leadership role to ensure all voices are heard during rehearsal. Co-leadership implies that each member equally contributes when playing together.

Curiosity—There is always something to learn from our musical colleagues, the score, and the context in which great art is created. Curiosity opens the door to exploration, experimentation, and co-creativity.

PART I

COLLABORATION BASICS TO BUILD YOUR TEAM

The Cavani Quartet's rehearsal techniques have defined chamber music for generations of artists. What an incredible legacy!
Amy Schwartz Moretti, Director of The McDuffie Center for Strings, Concert Violinist, and member Ehnes String Quartet

In Part I:

Chapter 1: Our Rehearsal and Teaching Philosophy
Chapter 2: Working Well Together

This part lays the foundation for creating a positive environment for learning and artistry. Successful collaboration involves open-mindedness, a willingness to try new ideas, and the joy of discovery. In the words of the Pulitzer Prize–winning poet and author Maya Angelou, "All great artists draw from the same resource: the human heart, which tells us we are more alike than unalike."[1]

The first chapter details our teaching philosophy representing foundational strategies and techniques for productive, fulfilling rehearsals. Elements of this philosophy include creating a positive environment for learning through empathy, humor, and co-leadership.

The second chapter addresses tension and conflict within groups, including strategies for working well together and creating a healthy environment for rehearsals and performances. These fundamental skills, combined with the rehearsal techniques and strategies, heighten the excellence of your ensemble.

1

OUR REHEARSAL AND TEACHING PHILOSOPHY

> Neither a lofty degree of intelligence nor imagination nor both together go to the making of genius. Love, love, love, that is the soul of genius.
>
> ~ Attributed to W. A. Mozart

In This Chapter:

- Working With Love and Inspiration
- The Importance of Relationships
- Creating a Positive Environment

Working with Love and Inspiration

> As a performer, giving of yourself and connecting with your audience involves communicating and inspiring and being inspired by your colleagues as well. As a teacher, I encourage each student to find their own voice to express the music in the most meaningful way.
>
> ~ Peter Salaff, former member, Cleveland String Quartet

The philosophy which underpins this book is based on three key elements: love, inspiration, and relationships (see Figure 1.1). These three elements form the environment in which interpretation and expression can flourish during performances. The rehearsal techniques at the center enable a productive and thriving work environment.

Love

Though not often spoken about, love is at the core of what we do in a healthy and thriving ensemble. Discipline, repetition, good individual practice habits, and spending time in productive rehearsals are all rooted in love. Chamber musicians are motivated to improve, centered on our love of the art form.

The Art of Collaboration. Annie Fullard and Dorianne Cotter-Lockard, Oxford University Press. © Oxford University Press 2025. DOI: 10.1093/oso/9780197673126.003.0002

12 The Art of Collaboration

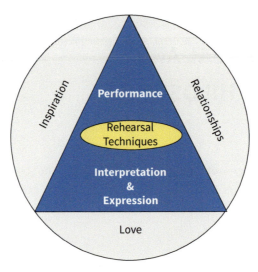

FIGURE 1.1 Art of Collaboration chamber music philosophy.

When we talk about love, we are not implying romance; we intend it to mean "strong predilection, liking, or fondness (for something); devotion (to something)."[1] Love can also mean connection with, value, and respect for our fellow human beings. We support each other through music and view chamber music playing as a microcosm of human relationships. Applying this philosophy through relationship-building techniques can lead to a transformative chamber music rehearsal and performance process.

Stories have circulated about string quartets with dysfunctional relationships and tense or even negative working environments. From time to time, there are circumstances where conflicts within ensembles cannot be resolved.

With the right tools and guidance, ensemble groups can work through most conflicts with ease and understanding and even learn to prevent conflicts before they arise. The Cavani Quartet was fortunate to learn from a variety of teachers and mentors, including those from the Borodin, Juilliard, Cleveland, Tokyo, Colorado, and Emerson string quartets, who demonstrated mutual respect and love for their colleagues.

Inevitably, heated discussions and disagreements about musical decisions are a part of the rehearsal process. To transform these discussions into productive conversations, the Cavani Quartet developed a set of techniques to resolve conflicts and enable respectful communication among ensemble members, which we present in this book. We encourage you to approach rehearsals and your colleagues with a loving attitude.

Inspiration

Inspiration comes from the music, our colleagues, teachers and coaches, the audience, and our environment. Music is a source of energy that transports us into a

FIGURE 1.2 Peter Salaff coaching students at Cleveland Institute of Music.

realm beyond words. We fall in love with each piece of music as we learn and perform it. The more we perform a piece, the more intense our relationship with it becomes, like a deepening friendship. As we search for inspiration in music, we reflect internally to draw upon our own experience and imagination.

We draw inspiration from our colleagues through mutual respect and collaboration. One idea can be powerful, but the amalgamation of multiple ideas is transformative. We prevent dissension and conflict in rehearsal by adopting an attitude of collective learning and inspiration.

The coach or teacher has a responsibility to inspire and encourage ensembles to think about the creative process. A motivating coach can help an ensemble find their voice as artists and interpreters (see Figure 1.2).

Take inspiration from your audience as if they were a member of the ensemble. As musicians, we find fulfillment through sharing a common bond of beauty and pathos with our listeners. Feeling reciprocal love and energy from the audience can be electrifying.

The Importance of Relationships

> The thing I think I love most about chamber music is that it is fundamentally about collaborating with other humans. Every moment of ensemble playing involves some sort of relationship with another person—be it a colleague or an audience member. I find this to be such a powerful space; it is a domain that encourages tremendous growth.
> ~ Elizabeth Oakes, violist, Director, University of Iowa String Quartet Program, former member of the Maia Quartet

14   The Art of Collaboration

One of the inspirations for this book originates from Annie's experience as a member of the Cavani Quartet. Being a part of this ensemble profoundly affected her life and approach to music-making. In her words:

> One of the experiences in my life that I am most grateful for is the time spent with my colleagues in the Cavani Quartet. The Quartet's first decade was filled with rich learning and performing opportunities, and I would not trade those formative experiences for the world. Our rehearsals were initially fraught with difficulties navigating our lives as college students and managing group dynamics. While we always had an appreciation for each other and a deep respect and love for music, we often faced challenges communicating our anxieties and concerns related to the group's rehearsal process. Let's say the tears flowed, and the occasional door was slammed. These feelings and challenges can be typical for young and developing ensembles. These experiences underlined my belief that forging healthy relationships within an ensemble is as important as addressing the technical aspects of performing a piece of music.
>
> Out of necessity, the Cavani Quartet created strategies to cultivate a positive and joyful work environment, including an abundance of humor. Along the way, the quartet developed specific rehearsal techniques which unified our approach and diffused conflict. As we grew into our roles as teachers, we noticed how these strategies and techniques enabled our student ensembles to be more responsive, connected, and productive. It is my life's joy to celebrate the creativity of my musical peers and colleagues. I remain buoyed by the endless joy of discovery in music and the never-ending opportunities to learn and share. (Annie Fullard)

Artistic fulfillment and success in an ensemble include not only becoming a highly skilled musician but also cultivating healthy communication, positive relationships, and personal happiness. As authors of this book, we aim to help others share this philosophy.

Creating a Positive Environment

> Begin with a positive comment or enthusiastic observation because that creates an atmosphere of respect. As a result, people will be open and ready to learn together . . . powerful music-making can unfold on its own if these basic communication practices are in place.
>
> ~ Mari Sato, former member, Cavani String Quartet

In This Section:
• Respectful Communication
• Empathy
• Playfulness, Joy, and Laughter
• Co-Leadership

In this section, we underline our philosophy with guidance in four areas which support the overall theme of collaboration. These four elements serve as motives woven like threads throughout the book to create a positive rehearsal environment.

Respectful Communication

Respectful communication among ensemble members provides the groundwork for a positive team environment. Neuroscience and physiology research demonstrates that negative or frequent criticism does not work well in a learning environment. On the contrary, recent studies indicate that positive communication and collaboration elicit positive emotional states within individuals, resulting in openness to new ideas, active cooperation, and willingness to change behaviors in a group setting.[2]

We first acknowledge the successful aspects of the rehearsal or performance to create a positive ensemble environment. Maintaining this environment requires a balance of being sensitive to others and expressing one's own voice. During Dorianne's research, one of our chamber music students observed, "It's amazing how sensitive you really do have to be to other people . . . to accommodate them without surrendering too much of your own personal voice, finding a way to make all that work together."[3]

Empathy

> You can console each other empathetically in moments of sadness in the music. Through the music you're sensing and feeling each other's pain and embracing each other, so you express that feeling together. There's a sense of humanity or family in it.
> ~ Peter Salaff, former member, Cleveland String Quartet

In addition to practicing respectful communication, developing empathy is essential for chamber musicians. To be the most effective ensemble member means not only understanding the pain and joy of the composer, music, and fellow musicians but also being aware of the audience and humanity.

When you are empathetic, it is easier to communicate with care, show respect, and express kindness toward others. You develop a greater understanding of how your fellow musicians may be thinking and feeling, and you come to appreciate your commonalities and differences more over time, thus decreasing the likelihood of conflict.

By approaching your colleagues from a place of understanding and empathy, you build a sense of psychological safety among your group members. According to Harvard researcher Amy Edmonson, the concept of *psychological safety* is defined as "a shared belief that the team is safe for interpersonal risk taking."[4] Ensemble members take risks by expressing their ideas and trying out each other's ideas. It is essential to the rehearsal process to allow risk-taking in an environment that promotes creative thought.

Playfulness, Joy, and Laughter

The group that laughs together plays well together (see Figure 1.3). Infusing a sense of humor and playfulness into rehearsal adds richness to the musical experience and helps rehearsals flow with far greater ease. Humor is a powerful tool for diffusing tension and creating a positive atmosphere. While coaching and teaching, Annie will often shift the mood through a joke or pun. Here is one of her favorites: "Why couldn't Mozart find his friend? Because he was Haydn."

On a deeper level, having a sense of humor in rehearsal can serve to make everyone feel comfortable, set a tone of empathy, and allows for the expression of frustration without meanness or sarcasm. Noted *Wall Street Journal* theater critic, the late Terry Teachout explains the power of comedy and humor as follows:[5]

> As I grow older, I grow more firmly convinced that comedy is truer to life than tragedy, not just onstage but in all the narrative art forms. . . . It was Donald Francis Tovey, the noted English musicologist, who best explained why comedy has the potential to express more fully than tragedy the fundamental truths of life. In an essay about Mozart, Mr. Tovey pointed out that the language of such "tragic" masterpieces as the G Minor Symphony is derived from the rush and bustle of 18th-century opera buffa, abstracted to the point of sublimity but still fundamentally comic. . . . Mr. Tovey explained it: "Comedy uses the language of real life; and people in real life often find the language of comedy the only dignified expression for their deepest feelings."

In the next chapter, we provide examples illustrating how humor can be a sustaining ingredient in the rehearsal process.

FIGURE 1.3 Cavani Quartet—Laughter. (Photo credit: Robert Muller)

Co-Leadership

> The Omer Quartet owes a huge deal of gratitude and respect to the Cavani Quartet, who taught us how to make 1+1+1+1 equal infinity.
>
> ~ Alex Cox, cellist, former member, Omer String Quartet,
> current member, Thalia Quartet

It is paramount to encourage everyone to take a leadership role in the ensemble. Co-leadership implies a balance of responsibilities between ensemble members. Each person commits to individual preparation prior to rehearsal. In addition, members actively participate in making musical decisions and organizational activities. Members should hold each other accountable for creating a rehearsal atmosphere in which every individual contributes their ideas and are willing to try the ideas of others.

We move beyond the traditional concepts of "leading" and "following" by introducing the concepts of *initiating, inspiring*, and *reflecting*. *Initiating* corresponds to cueing, ensemble members *inspire* each other, and *reflecting* is a response to initiation and inspiration. These concepts are explored more deeply in later chapters of the book.

2

WORKING WELL TOGETHER

> I think, team first. It allows me to succeed, it allows my team to succeed.
>
> ~ LeBron James

In This Chapter:

- Foundations to Build the Collaborative Team
- Causes of Tension and Conflict
- Strategies for Working Well Together

Foundations to Build the Collaborative Team and Create a Positive Environment

> A good collaboration is one in which musicians build each other up by mutual strengthening towards a common goal. It's a little like climbing a mountain. You go up first, and then you pull me up, and then I'll go the next leg and I'll pull you up.
>
> ~ David Finckel, Artistic Co-Director of the Chamber Music Society of Lincoln Center, former member, Emerson String Quartet

In This Section:
- Appreciation
- Inquiry and Invitation
- Listening
- Energy
- Collaborative Dialogue

What does it take to work well together? Chamber music can be the ultimate democracy—where all voices are heard, and all experiences respected. But achieving this involves mutual intention among all players and mindful practice in building a team that collaborates more and conflicts less. Respect and listening to all perspectives during rehearsal results in a heightened musical conversation during performances. Creating a positive environment is the first step in building a collaborative team.

Research has shown that positive dialogue affects our brain and nervous system, helping us become open to change and possibility.[1] Critical thinking and implementing improvements are essential to the rehearsal process, and open dialogue facilitates a higher caliber of playing. Traditionally, classical musicians have a pattern of leading conversations during rehearsals with criticism, often resulting in frustration and miscommunication. While there are ways to frame

The Art of Collaboration. Annie Fullard and Dorianne Cotter-Lockard, Oxford University Press. © Oxford University Press 2025. DOI: 10.1093/oso/9780197673126.003.0003

criticism that can block improvement, there are also strategies to present constructive critiques.

It is critical to learn and practice communicating with diplomacy versus derision. Rehearsals sometimes trigger defensiveness, anger, or withdrawal from the conversation. Stories have circulated regarding famous string quartets, such as the Guarneri and Budapest, who often did not travel together—not because they did not get along, but rather to allow for self-care and recharging. According to Arnold Steinhardt of the Guarneri Quartet, "people seemed to need to believe that the four members of a string quartet, living in blissful harmony, do everything together, and when its members don't, theories of strife, intrigue, and conspiracy spring to life." Steinhardt added that a "certain amount of private time was like a battery charge to be expended at quartet sessions."[2]

The techniques in this book preempt nonproductive and negative rehearsal behaviors before they occur. This section includes four strategies to create a positive rehearsal environment: appreciation, inquiry and invitation, listening, and energy. The combination of these strategies empowers group members to co-create a healthy working atmosphere.

Appreciation

> Teamwork is being sensitive to each other's creative freedom . . . to bring something to the table and at the same time be receptive to what everyone else is suggesting . . . to create something that is bigger than any individual.
> ~ Alex Cox, cellist, Thalea Quartet

A positive working environment starts with acknowledging an appreciation of group performance and individual contributions. Even something as simple as greeting each other in a friendly manner at the beginning of rehearsals helps establish mutual respect and appreciation.

Setting the tone at the beginning of the rehearsal with a positive observation before moving to suggestions for improvement reduces stress and results in greater productivity. Here are a few guidelines for expressing appreciation:

✓ Once you play through a section or movement, make your first comments about what may have worked well or a section you felt was successful as a group. For example, "We really nailed the crazy rhythm at letter B!"

✓ Make your comments specific, for example, "Eric, the opening viola theme was really striking and beautiful. I loved the amazing color at the very end. Could we play that passage again, paying attention and matching the color of Eric's sound?"

✓ Use language that you feel comfortable with so that your appreciation is accepted as genuine.

Inquiry and Invitation

Inquiry sets the stage for open dialogue. Rather than making a demand or statement, asking questions with the intention of discovery allows group members to remain open rather than become defensive. Before asking questions or making suggestions, invite your colleagues to offer theirs. For example, you might say, "Who has a spot they want to work on?" Every personality in the group has a different way of processing and expressing suggestions. Creating a space of invitation allows everyone an opportunity to contribute.

Ask questions and be curious about your colleagues' ideas and thought processes. We encourage you to ask open questions. Avoid asking closed questions unless fact-checking (answers are yes/no, or a specific answer). Use phrases like, "What if we tried _____?" or "I wonder if we could try this [idea here]?"

Open Questions and Statements
- ✓ What . . . ?
- ✓ What if . . . ?
- ✓ How do you . . . ? How could we . . . ?
- ✓ Tell me about . . . . I'm curious about . . . .
- ✓ Tell me more . . . .

Closed Questions
- ✓ Is it . . . ?
- ✓ Are you . . . ?

Avoid (can cause others to be defensive):
- ✓ Why did/do you . . . ?
- ✓ Judgmental statements, such as "you're not with me."

Listening

> My advice is to listen to each other. I don't mean instrumentally; I mean to people's ideas. Listening to people's ideas with respect is the first and foremost thing to successful rehearsing.
> ~ Tom Rosenberg, President, Fischoff Chamber Music Competition

Learning when to listen rather than talk is a powerful skill. Andrew Yee, cellist of the Attacca Quartet, suggests leaving space in the silence for people to speak. When silence occurs, Yee asks internally, "Do I enter the silence with my idea? Or do I not?" Yee adds, "Over the course of my 20 years with the quartet, I no longer need to fill the silence. Instead, we say, 'Can we play it again? And think of this concept?'"

Listening is also an essential leadership skill—one which Dorianne emphasized in her commencement speeches to each graduating class of new supervisors in her executive role within a corporation. The topic of her speech was "The Three L's"—*learning, listening,* and *loving.* The main points were that we never stop learning, listening is a critical aspect of communication, and loving your work and the people you work with engages the team toward a common goal.

Communication is a key competency of teamwork, and listening is at least 50 percent of healthy communication. The Greek philosopher Diogenes is attributed with saying, "We have two ears and only one tongue so that we would listen more and talk less." Steven Covey said, "Seek first to understand, then to be understood."[3]

Active listening is key to negotiation—if a person with a different idea feels understood, they'll be more likely to compromise.[4] By active listening, we mean that in addition to focusing your attention on the speaker during your rehearsal discussions, reflect back to the speaker what you heard to ensure you understood them correctly.

Body language also plays a pivotal role. When listening to ensemble members, consider adopting a stance of positive energy and encouragement. As you communicate your ideas, be aware of how your words affect your colleagues by observing their body language. This nuanced interaction between colleagues is a critical team building component.

Energy

Individual energy levels can affect the vibe of the rehearsal negatively or positively. Like athletes, musicians must be mindful of their physical state. Caring for your health and wellness as a musician includes warming up on your instrument and stretching your body before rehearsing. Cavani Quartet cellist Kyle Price hosts a program called *Your Body Is Your Strad* (http://www.yourbodyisyourstrad.com). In the following passage, he speaks to the process of engaging a somatic perspective during rehearsals (Box 2.1).

To maintain energy, also plan for stretch and snack breaks during rehearsals. In the Cavani Quartet, caffeine plays an important part in lifting our energy levels. Annie even travels with her personal coffee maker (it has its own suitcase). We also keep a well-stocked kitchen to prevent crankiness.

During the rehearsal, it is important to be aware of your posture and body language, especially when not playing. Always give your full attention to the creative process—we recommend you try not to yawn, slouch, text, or *kvetch*.[5]

Box 2.1 Engaging Somatic Awareness

Listening and learning from our bodies allows us to widen our awareness and provides more options to enjoy creative flexibility in our playing. Often one hears about feeling "stuck," which stems from a sense of not having options. Through somatic methods (e.g., Feldenkrais, Alexander, yoga), we can better understand our inner connection and apply countless options to playing our instrument and life. Options create choice, and choice allows creative and personal freedom.

The Feldenkrais Method deepens our awareness through physical and mental *differentiation*. One example is the Chamber Music Aerobics rehearsal technique. We externalize the pulse through movements up and down, side to side, and circularly. Therefore, we create options for expressing music to each other and deepening our internal and external connectivity.

I warm up with a series of mental and physical differentiation exercises away from and at the instrument. An example can be as simple as a *bow crawl* from the Suzuki method (walking our fingers up and down the bow) or another quick favorite, putting your hand on the balance point of the bow, and bowing an open string to the tip and back all the way to the frog (yes, past your hand)! Do this a few times. Then move your hand to its normal position at the frog and take a full bow. Does anything feel different?

Focus on listening internally and approaching your warmup exercises with curiosity. Observe the results, whether good, bad, or something else. There are no wrong answers, only awareness. These tools for deepening our listening and empathy toward ourselves are essential for bringing positive and playful energy to the rehearsal and performance process.

Collaborative Dialogue

> Respect is the key to successful collaboration, to have respect for everyone in the ensemble. It doesn't mean that you'll agree with all their ideas. But respect as the bottom line is crucial.
>
> ~ Martha Strongin Katz, former violist, Cleveland String Quartet

Engaging in constructive dialogue requires practice—much like you would slowly practice a passage of music to get it into your muscle memory. When offering comments, try these three steps:

1. Acknowledge what was successful in a musical passage that you feel was well-played.

Working Well Together   23

2. Invite your colleagues to try a passage or phrase that you feel needs improvement, clearly stating what you would like to work on.
3. Choose a character word or adjective that inspires your colleagues to understand your objective.

For example, you might say, "The tempo at the opening of this movement felt comfortable and flowed nicely. Could we try the transition into the development? I feel like I could line up better with the cello part, and I was wondering if we could play more rhythmic intensity and slightly louder there. I feel this section has an anxious quality which moves us forward. Can we try that together?"

More constructive dialogue examples are provided in Box 2.2 to incorporate into your collaborative conversation skills.

Box 2.2 Constructive Dialogue Examples

Be constructive: Critique the performance, not the person. Tone of voice makes all the difference on how your comments and questions are received. Consider using an open and objective tone.

- ✓ Rather than saying to your colleague, "You were out of tune at letter B!," you could say, "Could we work on intonation at letter B?"
- ✓ Instead of saying, "You're not with me," you might say, "It seems like we're not playing together here" or "I don't feel like I'm with you in this passage. Can we try it again?" Then, use one of the rehearsal techniques from this book.
- ✓ For a productive way to match articulations, you might say, "I would like to match your articulation better in measure 27. Could you demonstrate how you play that?"
- ✓ After they demonstrate it, you could say, "Now can we try that together?" If you have a different interpretation, ask if you can demonstrate, and again ask to try your idea with your colleague. Then, discuss it as a group and be open to suggestions.
- ✓ After playing through a passage, you might say, "I really liked the way we handled the transition to the recapitulation. Could we try it again and exaggerate the dynamic contrast? Could we try it out at letter C, so the soft passage is more extraordinary?"

Causes of Tension and Conflict

One needs the ability to be aware . . . to know if a comment is going too far or is too personal, to be able to sense when you need to back off a little bit, in fact to know when you shouldn't say anything.

~ Merry Peckham, former cellist, Cavani Quartet

> **In This Section:**
>
> - Blaming or Personalizing
> - Taking Things Personally
> - Lack of Focus
> - Misunderstandings and Assumptions
> - Strongly Held Views
> - Not Following Through

Conflict within an ensemble can result from a variety of causes. We mention a few of the most common causes of conflict here so you can identify these circumstances as they arise. We offer some solutions to address each of these causes.

Blaming or Personalizing

Blaming can be a way to avoid taking responsibility for one's words or actions, like, "You said x, so I did it that way." Another form of blaming, such as "you caused us to slow down there," is an unhelpful way to express an opportunity for improvement because it calls out an individual person. This type of blaming personalizes the issue, triggering negative emotions and causing stress hormones to flow in the accused person's body. Studies show that stress hormones shut down the frontal cortex part of the brain (the reasoning part) and receptivity to try a new idea or make a change.[6]

An emotionally and socially mature person takes full responsibility for their behavior. They are honest in admitting when they make a mistake or say something that is hurtful to another person. They avoid blaming others when something goes wrong. They take a moment to think before they speak, consider their words carefully, and monitor their tone of voice.

These are critical skills for creating a healthy collaborative environment. Use the dialogue examples from earlier in this chapter to express ideas and challenges without adding blame or personalizing your comments.

Taking Things Personally

Imagine someone said, "You caused us to slow down there." They could have expressed this more helpfully, but they did not. You have a choice to take it as a personal attack or not. Our own internal critic may already berate us for making a mistake or slowing down the tempo. If people already hear this voice, they will likely be more sensitive to others' unskillful remarks.

A healthier approach is neither to berate ourselves nor take things personally when another person is critical. In his book of Toltec wisdom, *The Four Agreements*, Don Miguel Ruiz[7] states that the second agreement is "Do not take anything personally." People can be unskillful in their communication. By adopting an open attitude of not taking things personally, you can prevent yourself from shutting down or building up resentment.

Lastly, redirect conversations by saying something like, "Let's focus on improving this passage by using a specific technique." Then, try a few techniques in Part IV to resolve the specific challenge.

Lack of Focus

A lack of focus can show up in different ways. For example, one or two group members might take the discussion completely off track by talking about something unrelated to the topic. In this case, you can gently suggest, "Let's return to the question/musical phrase we are exploring" or remind the group of the remaining time to achieve your planned goals for that day. If the conversation is relevant for a future discussion, write it down and agree to talk about it at a specified time.

In another example, a group member may arrive at rehearsal with something on their mind, such as an idea for a piece of music or something personal and cannot put it aside. Here, you could encourage them to talk about it briefly and consciously choose to put it aside. In her work with clients, Dorianne invites teams to start their meetings with a process called *clearing*, which she learned from her colleagues at Creating Extraordinary Organizations (CEO[2]). Each person states what is on their mind when they walk in the meeting room and affirms, "I choose to put it aside during the time of our meeting." This process respects the wholeness of each person—acknowledging that multiple aspects of our lives affect us in our work environment.

Others may tend to daydream during rehearsals and "zone out" when someone is making suggestions. If this becomes a pattern, address the habit in a private conversation between that person and one group member.

Misunderstandings and Assumptions

Misunderstandings often occur when assuming one knows what another person is thinking or feeling, or their motivation for doing or saying something. People make assumptions about what happened, what is planned, or even what was intended. The longer one waits to distinguish assumptions from the facts, the wider the gap between their understanding and the other person's. This can cause a variety of negative emotions among all concerned parties.

The best way to avoid misunderstandings is to adopt an attitude of curiosity through inquiry. You can ask clarifying questions such as, "I want to clarify something you said. I thought I heard x. Is that what you intended?" Ask further questions, such as "tell me more about that idea" or "I'm not sure I understand, what do you mean by y?" Test your assumptions directly: "I assumed x, is that correct, or am I mistaken?" "I assumed we agreed on y, did I misunderstand?" Keep asking these types of questions without blaming or personalizing until you have reached a collective understanding.

Strongly Held Views

Holding onto one's own viewpoint is arguably the most common cause of tension and conflict within a music ensemble. It is normal to be passionate about music, and people often have unique ways in which they interpret and express musical ideas. Group members can learn to share strong viewpoints while respecting other's perspectives. The most effective strategy for negotiating strongly held views is one that our professional colleagues and mentors employ: implement each idea as it is articulated before offering a different idea. You are encouraged to adopt the philosophy and practices of *Try Every Idea as if It Were Your Own* (we devote a section in this chapter to this strategy) and our capstone technique: *Live, Breathe, and Die* (*LBAD*).

Professional chamber music ensembles have their own decision-making approaches related to interpretation. The Budapest Quartet used a unique democratic voting process. According to biographer Nat Brandt, for each piece, one of the four members would have a second "composer's vote" decided by a random drawing of matchsticks—three short and one long. The quartet member who chose the long matchstick got the second vote.[8]

This approach illustrates how each ensemble will develop their own process for making musical decisions. We explain decision-making options in greater detail in the "Respecting Different Personalities" section of this chapter.

Not Following Through

Organization responsibilities should be equally distributed between group members. Resentments can build up when one person takes on too many responsibilities or another does not follow through on the tasks they agreed to take on. The expectation is that when an ensemble member agrees to do something, they follow through. This could include learning one's part and the score, researching, making a phone call, or arranging a rehearsal location.

It is best to separate discussion about ensemble logistics and management concerns from rehearsal sessions. Hold regular, short meetings to make agreements, update each other on progress toward agreed-upon actions, and make plans. Roles, responsibilities, and agreements within ensembles are discussed in Chapter 5, "Rehearsal Playbook"

Strategies for Working Well Together

When the Juilliard Quartet did open rehearsals, people would talk about "the nuclear Juilliard Quartet"—that all Hell was breaking loose. It was intense with a lot of fast talking, but if you listened carefully, there was not a single thing personal going on with any of it. It was all about the music, with passion, but nothing negative, ever.

~ Earl Carlyss, former member, Juilliard Quartet

This section includes strategies for working well together based on the Cavani Quartet's experience and Dorianne's research and professional expertise as an organizational leader, coach, and consultant.

> **In This Section:**
>
> - Try Every Idea as if It Were Your Own
> - Rule of Agreement
> - Compromise Equals Improvement
> - Laugh Together, Play Together
> - Respect Personalities
> - Emotional Intelligence
> - Bring Your Best Self

Try Every Idea as if It Were Your Own

Try Every Idea as if It Were Your Own is a foundational practice, inspired by the Cavani Quartet's mentor, Peter Salaff, former second violinist, Cleveland String Quartet, and the other former members of the Cleveland String Quartet. Here is an excerpt of our interview with Donald Weilerstein, former first violinist, Cleveland String Quartet, which explains the underlying philosophy and practice (Box 2.3).

Box 2.3 Sage Advice from Donald Weilerstein, Former Member, Cleveland String Quartet

---

There are a variety of ways to work in a rehearsal. You want to try each other's ideas because it has to do with mutual respect. It is important to respond respectfully, rather than saying "I just can't do that" without even trying the idea by playing it with the utmost commitment. Try your best to make the idea work. When you try the idea, the person who suggested it feels they had a voice in the rehearsal process. That is such an important thing in quartet psychology.

One thing that saves a lot of time is if the person demonstrates their idea by playing rather than trying to explain it.

If an idea is not accepted by the quartet, what do you do about it? We found it worked the best when we tried to amalgamate an idea, or a portion of the idea, into what we were already doing. It often made it sound better. Everyone really felt that they were contributing to the result.

Earl Carlyss (former Juilliard String Quartet [JSQ] second violinist) told a famous story to the Cavani Quartet about the JSQ as they struggled to agree on an interpretation of a Mozart quintet. Dorianne had the privilege of hearing the same story

28 The Art of Collaboration

during interviews with Earl Carlyss and Joel Krosnick, former members of the JSQ. According to violinist Earl Carlyss:

> It was the Mozart g minor viola quintet. The minuet movement [sings a few bars]. I felt that if it was too slow, the *sforzandos* would sound like cocker spaniels barking, and Bobby [Robert Mann] felt that if it was too fast, it lost a certain solemnity. The others for some reason didn't care. It was not that big a deal—it was not a life-or-death disagreement.
>
> And we had the option with two performances to play it one way the first night and the other way the second night. So, the first night we agreed to play it my way, a little faster. As we started it, I thought, "maybe Bobby is right." So, we played the minuet and then the trio, then we went back to the minuet. And by that time, I had decided that Bobby's way was better.
>
> After we finished the performance, we walked off stage, and before I could open my mouth, Bobby turned to me and said, "you know, I liked it that way." So, we had done a complete 180, both of us, in one performance.

Hearing the same story from two different JSQ members made it even more meaningful. Former JSQ cellist Joel Krosnick relayed his version of this story:

> My dear colleague Earl Carlyss used to say, "a terribly important part of playing chamber music is learning to play with equal conviction an idea or a conception of a sound or phrase which is not yours." I remember when we played the g minor Mozart viola quintet. We thoroughly worked out both ways of interpretation (Earl's and Bobby's) of the minuet movement. At the concert that followed those conversations, before we started the minuet, Mr. Mann turned to us and whispered, "which way?"

After hearing this story from Earl Carlyss, the Cavani Quartet felt inspired by the ability of these great artists to be so committed to each other that they would try different ideas with complete conviction. Our capstone rehearsal technique in Chapter 14, called *Live, Breathe, and Die (LBAD)*, evolved from this practice of *Try Every Idea as if It Were Your Own.*

Cavani Quartet members and our former and current students frequently use this technique to resolve differences of opinion. *LBAD*, combined with the *Rule of Agreement*, diffuses tension and resolves conflict when ensemble members hold strong views of their interpretation of the music.

Rule of Agreement from Comedy Theater Improv

> We had a rule in our group that we tried to receive comments as "yes, and . . ." responses. If somebody asked for something, even if it wasn't expected, we always tried to say, "yes, and we can do that. After that, can we try another idea?" We learned this from people who do stand-up comedy, who improvise

and make their imaginations move forward with their partner. Saying "yes, and . . ." every time refreshes the environment.

~ Ayane Kozasa, violist, Kronos Quartet,
former member Aizuri Quartet

The rule of agreement, described as "yes, and . . ." is used in improvisational comedy, where a participant accepts a statement from another ("yes") and builds on the idea ("and").[9] This technique is also used in business and other settings to enhance brainstorming sessions, promote active communication, and freely exchange ideas.

In rehearsal, practice using the rule of agreement as an immediate response to a musical inquiry from a colleague. This will create an open and friendly dialogue which avoids a contentious debate. The rule of agreement is a time saver and a conduit for healthy discussions that lead to creative solutions. Members of the ensemble will feel their idea has been heard and tried to the best of everyone's abilities.

Here is some improvisation advice excerpted from *Bossypants* by Tina Fey,[10] which serves as an example of the rule of agreement (Box 2.4). This guidance also applies to working together in chamber music groups:

"Yes, and . . ." creates a path to receptive attitudes during rehearsals. Humor adds a dimension of ease to this receptivity, further enhancing the rehearsal process.

Box 2.4 Tina Fey: Rule of Agreement

The first rule of improvisation is AGREE. Always agree and SAY YES. When you're improvising, this means you are required to agree with whatever your partner has created.

Now, obviously in real life you're not always going to agree with everything everyone says. But the Rule of Agreement reminds you to 'respect what your partner has created' and to at least start from an open-minded place. Start with a YES and see where that takes you.

The second rule of improvisation is not only to say yes, but YES, AND. You are supposed to agree and then add something of your own. . . . if I say, "I can't believe it's so hot in here," and you say, "What did you expect? We're in Hell," . . . now we're getting somewhere.

To me YES, AND means don't be afraid to contribute. It's your responsibility to contribute. Always make sure you're adding something to the discussion. Your initiations are worthwhile.

Compromise Equals Improvement

It is our experience with chamber music, *compromise equals improvement*, meaning that when you amalgamate another's idea with your own, you end up with a better

30 The Art of Collaboration

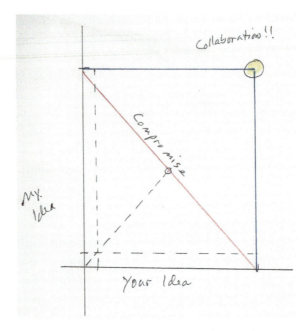

FIGURE 2.1 Compromise vs. collaboration. (by James Dunham and Warren Dunham)

result. Trying someone else's idea with conviction strengthens your creative process and leads to true collaboration. James Dunham, former violist of the Cleveland Quartet, during his interview with us, provided a diagram based on a conversation with his brother, business consultant Warren Dunham, about the difference between compromise and collaboration (see Figure 2.1).

Laugh Together, Play Together

The rehearsal process requires focus and a serious approach. However, an injection of humor balances the work effort. The ensemble that laughs together performs better together. Humor is one of the best antidotes to release tension during rehearsal. Silliness and laughter can open the door to experimentation or a relaxation response, allowing ensemble members to play with greater ease.

Finding opportunities to get together outside rehearsals can be enjoyable, like sharing a meal. In our formative touring days, the Cavani Quartet would stop for breakfast and order everything on the menu to sample—we always finished every morsel! Annie's obsession was pancakes, and we would drive out of our way to find the best pancake house.

This story about Budapest Quartet members having fun together during rehearsal shows how silliness and laughter can help a group diffuse a frustrating moment: (Box 2.5).[11]

Working Well Together   **31**

> ### Box 2.5 Budapest Quartet: Sense of Humor
>
> The Quartet members also realized how important it was to relieve the tensions of constant tours and travel. Once in a while at a rehearsal, just for the fun of it, they switched chairs—Boris [the violist] playing first violin; Mischa [cellist], second violin; Joe [first violinist], the viola; and Sasha [second violinist], the cello. Sasha once discovered a bass drum and set of cymbals, both with foot pedals, in the corner of the studio during an exasperating recording session. He lugged the drum to his chair, Boris got the cymbals, and they played the problem passage, banging away like crazed musicians. After hearing the playback of that organized chaos, they felt inspired to run through a few Russian dances, and then they recorded the troublesome passage without any difficulty.

Respect Personalities

People with different personality preferences use various approaches to receive communication and express themselves. Frager and Fadiman[12] define personality as an "individual pattern of thinking, feeling, and acting."

Many models have been developed to assess an individual's personality type.[13] By understanding basic information regarding your personality and those of others on your team, you can find ways to communicate better and resolve conflicts.

Some people like to process ideas by talking through them, while others prefer to spend time alone to think things through and come back to the group to discuss them. If someone in your group needs processing time before joining the discussion, try pausing after introducing a new idea, then come back together to discuss it.

In another example of personality differences, some people need more time to adjust to the prospect of making a change in plans or direction. Imagine that your ensemble has been presented with a new opportunity, such as a series of concerts requiring significant travel, or one of your members just accepted a position with a major orchestra. Perhaps one of your members hates to make quick decisions. You can alleviate tension in these scenarios by having an initial group conversation to identify the facts and options related to the situation and agreeing on a time to meet again to make a group decision. For these conversations, ensure everyone has equal time to express their opinions and ideas. With this approach, the quietest voice in the room may make the most valuable contribution to the group's decision process.

Lastly, some prefer to list all the pros and cons before they make a decision, while others use their "gut" or intuition. Here, respect each person's perspective and decision-making approach by listening carefully and remaining open to their ideas and opinions. Adopting an attitude of no one "right" answer may make it more likely to find a "third way" that works better than the initial solution.

32 The Art of Collaboration

One final aspect of personality to consider is the continuum between "flying by the seat of your pants" and planning every aspect of a group's activities. Be aware of this continuum and try the following actions:

- ✓ Spend some time getting to know each other's preferences regarding planning, decision-making, and communication.
- ✓ Talk about it from a position of curiosity and a desire to find successful communication methods for your group members.
- ✓ Adjust approaches depending on context. As your group spends more time working together and understanding each other's planning, decision-making, and communication styles, you may find a greater willingness to be flexible.

Emotional Intelligence

> The Golden Rule is crucial. Make comments to others as you would want others to make comments to you. It creates empathy, compassion and understanding of others.
>
> ~ Peter Salaff, former member, Cleveland String Quartet

In addition to learning how to play our instruments and how to approach learning a piece of chamber music, we need to effectively manage our emotions when working with others. According to Daniel Goleman, emotional intelligence (EQ) is "the capacity for recognizing our own feelings and those of others, for motivating ourselves, for managing emotions well in ourselves and in our relationships."[14] Studies show that leaders can dramatically affect the emotional state of group members, causing team members to be more or less receptive to new ideas and to change.[15] These studies corroborate our experience with students and colleagues in maintaining a positive, collaborative environment.

Figure 2.2 illustrates the three steps in developing emotional intelligence (EQ). The first step in developing your EQ is to recognize your emotions in the moment. Start

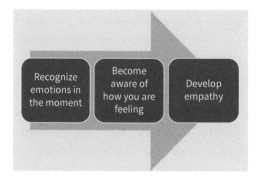

FIGURE 2.2 Steps to developing emotional intelligence.

by reflecting at the end of each day on the range of your emotions (positive and negative). Write them down—develop a wide vocabulary to express them. Next, practice checking in with yourself in the moment. What are the signs in your body that you are becoming frustrated or angry? Do you feel the temperature rise in your neck and face, or a tightness in your chest or shoulders? Some people breathe more shallowly when they are upset. Explore how you know you are feeling anger, frustration, or joy.

The second step is to become increasingly aware of how you are feeling. Once you do so, you can interrupt the negative emotion and use your EQ to express yourself effectively to your colleagues. If you do not interrupt the negative emotion in time, your amygdala and other parts of your emotional, reactive brain will take over and literally shut down your thinking brain (the cerebral cortex).[16] You need your cerebral cortex to effectively discuss different ideas and perspectives, and to find solutions to problems!

The third step is to develop empathy, or "the ability to understand the emotional make-up of other people" and "the skill in treating people according to their emotional reactions."[17] Empathy is required to develop social awareness and to maintain healthy relationships. In their book, *Emotional Intelligence 2.0*, Bradberry and Greaves[18] provide several strategies to develop one's social awareness and to better manage relationships: careful listening, step into another's shoes, acknowledge other's feelings, and show you care. These skills can be developed and used to enhance relationships among group members.

Bring Your Best Self

What can you do to ensure your behavior is at its best? First, embrace the attitude that you are responsible for your words, actions, and emotions. Together, decide how you can gently remind each other when someone does not appear to be taking responsibility for their behavior. Once you have an agreement, you can personally model constructive behaviors. When it appears that another person is not taking full responsibility for their behaviors, use the agreed-upon approach to remind them of the agreement. It might be as simple as saying, "Let's just try it." These are the only words that need to be spoken in the moment—otherwise, the conversation could turn into blaming.

Summary

The techniques in this book transform negative conflict into a positive problem-solving process. You will find a variety of primarily nonverbal techniques where everyone participates to resolve a musical or technical challenge. These techniques help diffuse and prevent tension and conflict. In addition to improving your ensemble's performance, the techniques in this book provide opportunities to laugh, enjoy the process, and have fun.

PART II

REHEARSAL PREPARATION AND PROCESS

Make sure that you emphasize you're getting the full capacity out of yourself as an instrumentalist, because you will have so much more freedom. Once you've done that, you can apply to your chamber music playing.
~ Peter Oundjian, former member, Tokyo String Quartet

In Part II:

Chapter 3: Individual Preparation
Chapter 4: Score Study
Chapter 5: Rehearsal Playbook

Part II offers best practices for individual preparation, including in-depth score study. Ensemble members set the stage for productive rehearsals when they arrive prepared to play their parts and have studied the score. Another method of preparation is to plan the repertoire and allocate blocks of time for each rehearsal. The "Rehearsal Playbook" chapter provides valuable strategies and an example of how to organize rehearsals.

3
INDIVIDUAL PREPARATION

> My advice is that everyone learns their part in the piece as well as possible before every rehearsal. Be prepared instrumentally and be open to discussing ideas.
> ~ Tom Rosenberg, President, Fischoff Chamber Music Competition

In This Chapter:

- Parts and Scores
- Practicing Your Individual Part
- Developing Your Interpretation
- What to Bring to Rehearsal
- Co-Leadership

Individual preparation is integral to a successful chamber music experience. When you play chamber music, think of yourself as a team member who is responsible for contributing as an equal partner. Approach your preparation with the following ideas in mind: play every note in your part with energy, purpose, and beauty, and clearly understand how your part fits into the whole (see Figure 3.1). Mindful preparation enables you to play with confidence and enhances your ability to connect in a more empathetic way with your colleagues. We offer a systematic approach to individual preparation for rehearsal.

FIGURE 3.1 Photo via Dorianne Cotter-Lockard.

Parts and Scores

Showing up with a well-organized and accessible part and score helps rehearsals run smoothly and ensures a positive working environment. Organizing your music can be done in one of two ways:

- ✓ A binder to organize the printed part and score helps with page turns and prevents your music from falling off the stand at inopportune moments (Box 3.1).
- ✓ A tablet to electronically store your parts and scores.

The Art of Collaboration. Annie Fullard and Dorianne Cotter-Lockard, Oxford University Press. © Oxford University Press 2025.
DOI: 10.1093/oso/9780197673126.003.0004

38   The Art of Collaboration

Make sure to organize your part and the score before the first rehearsal by acquiring the part and score and ensuring you have measure numbers. Taking these two steps demonstrates respect for your colleagues and the rehearsal process.

Box 3.1 Annie's Music!

Just about everyone has a music disaster story. Annie's worst music fiasco occurred when she put too much music in the binder. In the middle of a performance, the music stand fell over into the midst of the group, knocking over every else's stand. After a moment of awkward silence, she said to the audience, "this is *heavy* music."

Acquiring Parts and Scores

A multitude of resources are available to acquire parts and scores. Parts and scores are generally available free for download from websites such as www.IMSLP.org, or you can borrow a library part and score. You can also purchase them from various online sources (see Appendix A). In addition, ensemble members should work from the same edition of the music for consistency in notations, measure numbers, and section markers. For further guidance, see the chapter "Score Study."

Measure Numbers—Where Are We?

Measure numbers help with rehearsal time management, as individuals without measure numbers in their part often struggle to find the passage the group wishes to rehearse. Therefore, each ensemble member should write measure numbers in their part before the first rehearsal (if not already included). To accomplish this, mark the measure numbers at the beginning of each line of music in your part. Figure 3.2 shows an example of how to write measure numbers at the beginning of each line.

Note that the first and second endings count as the same measure number. Do not count the first ending when writing measure numbers in the part. For example, in

FIGURE 3.2 How to write measure numbers.

Figure 3.3, the measures in the first ending before the repeat do not receive measure numbers. The second ending is measure 127.

Once you have organized the basics regarding your part and score, you have set the stage for a productive and effective practice session.

FIGURE 3.3 Mendelssohn Octet for Strings in E-flat, Op.20, Allegro, first violin part.

Practicing Your Individual Part

It is important that chamber musicians allow themselves to grow as players, and that they have enough time to practice. They should practice individually so they can play well during rehearsal with the ensemble, at least an hour and a half to two hours of practice on their own. If this is not possible (e.g., while on tour or long hours of rehearsals), it is helpful to create a warmup routine utilizing basic technique. Practice challenging passages at moderate tempi, feeling a rhythmic pulse, and always giving yourself space through visualization.

~ Donald Weilerstein, former member, Cleveland String Quartet

Mindful individual practice is the cornerstone of impactful chamber music playing. We can draw inspiration from the experience of great athletes who drill and repeat individual skills to become a better team member. Individual preparation forges confidence and ease, helping you become a better collaborator. Technical perfection is not the objective—rather, it is about playing with ease, while focusing on other voices in the ensemble and musical expression. There are many techniques for developing solid individual practice habits and resources to aid in the process.

In This Section:

- Challenging Passages
- Repetition
- Rhythmic Variations
- Intonation
- Dynamics
- Rhythms
- The Metronome
- Beethoven's Tempo Markings
- Additional Hints

✓ Practice your part with energy and focus: place your full attention to the music and the passage you wish to improve. A sense of purpose, such as a small musical goal provides energy (as will a cup of espresso).
✓ Play every note with beauty (e.g., good intonation and a resonant sound) and musical intent (character, mood, and dynamics).
✓ Begin by practicing **slowly**. Renowned violinist Itzhak Perlman offers advice on slow practice in a series of videos called "Practicing Advice from Itzhak Perlman."[1]

The points above apply to all individual practice sessions. Gerald Klickstein calls this "artful practicing" in *The Musician's Way: A Guide to Practice, Performance, and Wellness*.[2] The following sections highlight techniques for practicing and solving different challenges.

Challenging Passages

If you practice slowly, you forget it slowly because the brain takes time to absorb it. The slower you do it, the better it is.

~ Itzhak Perlman

3. Scat or sing complex rhythms with syllables such as "la" or "da" instead of counting numbers.

Once you understand the rhythms by counting or scatting, the next step is to play the rhythms slowly and accurately. Gradually increase the tempo until you can play at the *tempo* indicated in the score.

In addition to learning the rhythms, make it a habit to practice breathing and cueing yourself in after every rest. A physical motion, like a conductor's cue, enables you to feel precise rhythm and ensures that everyone in your ensemble understands your intention (see the chapter "Cueing and Breathing").

The Metronome

Use the metronome as a practice partner. Playing with the metronome organizes technique and assists in feeling a strong rhythmic pulse. Practicing with the metronome helps you to be accurate when playing alone. However, once you join your ensemble in rehearsal it is important to be flexible. The following steps will aid your practice with the metronome.

1. Using the metronome, start with small subdivisions, which will enable rhythmic accuracy.
2. Try the metronome marking indicated by the composer. For example, Beethoven String Quartet, Op. 59. No. 1 (see Figure 3.4), set the metronome to quarter note subdivisions.
3. Move to larger subdivisions which allow for greater expressive freedom. Using the same example (see Figure 3.4), set the metronome to half-note subdivisions.
4. Move to whole note subdivisions.
5. Explore how it feels to use a larger pulse, which can help to create a longer line within a rhythmic framework. This enables flexibility and *rubato* within the small notes while maintaining a consistent larger pulse. Using the same example (Figure 3.4), set the metronome to pulse once every four measures.

A Note Regarding Beethoven's Tempo Markings

Beethoven's metronome marking for the first movement of String Quartet, Op. 59. No. 1, based on an article by Rudolf Kolisch,[4] is indicated as a half note = 88. This tempo marking is quite fast and is an indication of the character. Beethoven did not intend a rigid adherence to one *tempo* in his works, rather, the *tempo* marking gives an overview of the flow of the music (see the chapter "Score Study" for further information).

FIGURE 3.4 Beethoven String Quartet in C Major, Op.59, No. 1, Score.

Additional Helpful Hints

Below are a few additional hints to improve your practice habits and enhance the experience with your ensemble.

- ✓ Practice from the score to understand how your part fits in with the other parts.
- ✓ Warm up with scales in the key of your chamber music repertoire.
- ✓ Practice with the intent of playing passages from memory.
- ✓ Borrow a part for specific suggestions from a mentor, coach, or teacher.
- ✓ Ask your teacher or coach for a help session with your individual part.
- ✓ String players: practice passages using open strings with the indicated rhythm and dynamics without playing the notes.
- ✓ String players: practice *arco* passages using pizzicato to gain rhythmic clarity.

Developing Your Interpretation

In This Section:

- Exploring the Score
- Using Media as a Resource
- An Invitation to be Curious

Beginning the process of developing your interpretation of the work under study is an integral part of individual preparation. By engaging in the three activities in this section, you will be able to bring ideas to the interpretation discussion during rehearsals.

Exploring the Score

> The attitude of searching the depths of what is on the printed page is very important, without being a servant to the printed page.
>
> ~ Earl Carlyss, former member, Juilliard Quartet

The score is a vital tool for individual practice. By exploring the score, you deepen your appreciation and knowledge of the composer's intent and most importantly, how your part relates to the whole work, and to the other parts (see the chapter "Score Study").

- ✓ Write cues into your part which indicate rhythms or notes from other instruments.
- ✓ Highlight moments in the music when the ensemble plays all together, such as grand pauses, cadences, and unison passages.

Using Media as a Resource

> Broadus Erle was a strong believer in finding your own voice. One time, I was studying the 2nd Bartók Violin Sonata and I listened to a recording before I came in for my first lesson. After I played some of it, he didn't even hesitate when he asked, "did you listen to a recording of this?" He could tell right away that it was not coming from me, he could sense it.
>
> ~ Peter Salaff, former member, Cleveland String Quartet

Use a variety of media as a resource to observe how the other parts of your chosen repertoire relate to your own, and to guide you to make your own decisions about aspects of the music such as the sound quality, *tempo*, phrasing, and character.

Astrid Schween, cellist of the Juilliard String Quartet, suggests choosing a few different recordings of a movement and describing what you hear by making detailed notes in the score.

46   The Art of Collaboration

✓ Listen *actively* to recordings or videos and make notes about the specific interpretive aspects in the performance. A sort of interpretive diagram. This will give you an idea of different ways musicians interpret the same information.

✓ Listen to other works by the same composer or other composers of the same era, for context and perspective.

✓ Listen to recordings which feature the style or influences that inspired the composer. These could include folk or world music, jazz, rock, or unique instruments that are used in non-Western music.

Develop your *own* interpretation. Your observations of other artists' interpretations will inform your own ideas.

Composer Gabriela Lena Frank recommends listening to more than one interpretation of a contemporary work in addition to the recording by the premiering group if it is available. This practice expands the variety of ideas from which you draw inspiration (Box 3.2).

Box 3.2 Fall in Love with the Piece—Ways of Listening

✓ Listen with eyes closed.
✓ Listen while following the score.
✓ Listen while looking at your part.
✓ Listen with your imagination—visualize colors or a story that fits the music.
✓ Listen with your heart and emotions—how does the music make you feel?

An Invitation to Be Curious

Approach the work you are studying with curiosity—take the time to research and discover as much as possible. Learn about the social, political, and historical context. Learn about trends and styles in visual arts, architecture, dance, literature, and theater during the composer's era (see the chapter "Exploring the Composer's World").

✓ Discover when the piece was written.
✓ Look up all words that are unfamiliar and write the meanings in your part for reference.
✓ Learn about the personal story of the composer and the influence of other composers on their music.
✓ Bring a related fun fact to your first rehearsal or coaching session.

Attend as many live performances of chamber music as possible for inspiration!

What to Bring to Rehearsal (and Coaching Sessions)

Here are a few suggestions for organizing the tools you bring to rehearsals and coaching sessions. In addition to the items listed below, bring a sense of humor, adventure, and empathy to maintain a positive environment.

✓ Your part and the score in a binder or on a tablet with a pedal.
✓ A sharp pencil and eraser, or a stylus to write on your tablet.
✓ Instrument accessories, such as mutes, extra reeds, a cello stop, extra strings, rosin, etc.
✓ A portable, lightweight wire music stand, or a stand for your tablet is highly recommended for chamber music playing. We recommend adjusting your stand to a low height so you can connect easily with the other members of the ensemble.

Co-Leadership: Your Role in the Ensemble

Approach the individual preparation of your part with the expectation of having an equal leadership role in cueing and initiating and an equal voice in the artistic process. Co-leadership creates electricity across the ensemble and enables a more active musical conversation. Cavani Quartet members make it a goal to share the responsibility of cueing and initiating. This communication occurs through gesture which allows for spontaneous and creative music-making.

Each instrumental voice may serve different musical roles and functions (e.g., melody, harmony, subject, countersubject, rhythmic ostinato, or bass line). The ensemble benefits when each member understands their role and function and all members lead together through initiation of rhythm and sound. Co-leadership is an essential skill for collaboration. The rehearsal techniques offered in Part IV will help you to develop and incorporate this skill.

It is important to develop the qualities illustrated in Figure 3.5 to bring your best self to the ensemble. These qualities represent the ideal member of a high-functioning chamber music group, and include the following:

Supportive—as colleagues it is important to acknowledge each other's musical strengths and support each other's ideas and suggestions during the rehearsal process.

Inspirational—be inspired by the music and share your inspiration with your colleagues.

Honest—know yourself, and work to create a positive working atmosphere by communicating your ideas, feelings, and beliefs in a humble and respectful way.

48   The Art of Collaboration

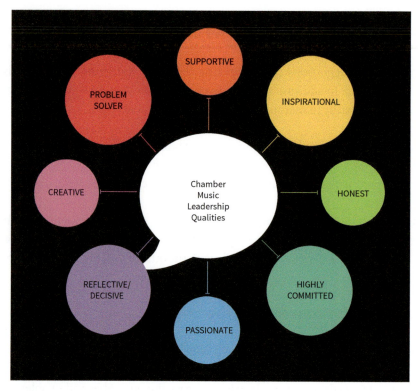

FIGURE 3.5 Chamber music leadership qualities.

Committed—follow through on mutual agreements, organizational responsibilities, and coordination, such as arriving on time for rehearsal and individual preparation.

Passionate—share your passion for the music and the process of learning together, show up with your full attention and energy.

Reflective and Decisive—practice mindful listening and engage fully during group dialogue to enable a healthy rehearsal process.

Creative—nurture your and your colleagues' creative process, allow ideas to emerge and evolve.

Problem-Solver—facilitate the successful exploration of solutions and the execution of everyone's ideas.

In this chapter, we provided several approaches to support individual preparation. These include recommendations to organize your part, to prepare the technical aspects, and to joyfully discover more about the music you will play. It is our experience that being prepared before you walk into the first rehearsal generates confidence and ease within each member and jump-starts the formation of the team. We also highlighted the importance of co-leadership and the qualities and behaviors that underpin successful co-leadership. In the next chapter, we present approaches to score study which further support individual and group preparation.

4
SCORE STUDY

One must have awareness of musical structure and musical relationships in the four-way, or more, conversation that goes on in chamber music.
~ Joel Krosnick, former member Juilliard String Quartet

In This Chapter:

- Editions of Parts and Scores
- Identifying Key Elements of the Score
- An Invitation to Play from the Score
- Have Fun with Your Score: An Exercise

Score study is fundamental to the rehearsal process and facilitates a deeper understanding of form, structure, melody, harmony, motivic development (rhythmic or melodic ideas repeated over different structures within a composition),[1] and dynamics. Studying the music from the perspective of the score helps visualize the contours of the music and pacing. The score reveals the structure of a musical composition—consider each musical phrase as a sentence. The sentences make up a paragraph, and the paragraphs lead to a fully realized composition.

The word *architecture* is also used when discussing musical structure—score study reveals how a composer creates small components to construct a beautiful whole. The joy of discovery through score study informs the interpretation approach and increases openness to different ideas when beginning rehearsal.

Editions of Parts and Scores

Using the same edition for your parts creates a more efficient rehearsal process and serves to unite your approach to musical decisions. Parts that have the same rehearsal numbers or letters save time when identifying a particular passage to work on. Within the same edition, notations, phrase markings, and articulations will be more consistent.

We also recommend you research different editions of the same score, which highlight various editors' points of view and can aid in the interpretive process. Different editions can aid your decision-making process for phrase markings and

The Art of Collaboration. Annie Fullard and Dorianne Cotter-Lockard, Oxford University Press. © Oxford University Press 2025.
DOI: 10.1093/oso/9780197673126.003.0005

FIGURE 4.1 Original manuscript, 4th movement, Mozart String Quartet in E-flat, K. 428.

articulations. If available, a copy of the original manuscript offers a window into the composer's intentions (see Figure 4.1).

We recommend starting with editions available from any of the following major publishers of music: Henle, Bärenreiter, Breitkopf & Härtel, Wiener Urtext, Peters, Boosey & Hawkes, SHAR Music, and Sikorski. These editions have been thoughtfully curated by various scholars and performing musicians.

You can obtain public domain music from International Music Score Library Project (IMSLP)-Petrucci Music Library (https://imslp.org). The website contains some interesting original editions. Resources for finding music of underrepresented composers are included in Appendix A.

For music of contemporary and living composers, honor the composer's copyright by purchasing the parts rather than using copies.

Identifying Key Elements of the Score

> I encourage students to study the scores, look at the overall structure of the music, the phrases, and to do harmonic analysis to give them the tools they need in order to bring the repertoire to life, and to communicate with and inspire each other and their audiences.
>
> ~ Peter Salaff, former member, Cleveland String Quartet

Score study is one of the most enlightening aspects of rehearsal preparation. The score offers a musical map to illuminate how individual parts fit into a cohesive whole. The ability to identify and note key musical elements listed in the box on this page will result in more productive and engaging rehearsals.

> **In This Section:**
>
> - Tempo and Character
> - Melodic Themes and Motives
> - Rhythmic Cues
> - Dynamics
> - Harmony
> - Form and Structure

Tempo and Character

The tempo and character markings are typically the first set of interpretive directions indicated by the composer. There will either be a tempo marking, a metronome marking, or both. Acknowledging the tempo and metronome markings at the beginning of each movement informs the interpretive process. An essential aspect of the rehearsal process is to understand all tempo markings and terminology in the score—research any term you do not fully understand. Online sources for musical terms include NAXOS Musical Terms Glossary, Wikipedia Glossary of Musical Terminology, Dictionary.com, and the Oxford Dictionary of Music.

- ✓ Carefully review the tempo marking at the beginning of every movement (e.g., *Allegro con brio*). The tempo marking provides clues to the intended character and mood.
- ✓ Research the definition and origin of the words indicating tempo and character. For example, *Andante* comes from the Italian word *andare*, which means "to go."
- ✓ If the composer indicates metronome markings in the score at the beginning of a movement, use them to guide the interpretive process.

The interpretation of terms related to tempo and character should be approached in the context in which they were written. For example, an *Adagio* composed by Johann Sebastian Bach would be interpreted differently than an *Adagio* composed by Gustav Mahler because of stylistic differences between the seventeenth century and the late nineteenth century. The metronome was not invented until the nineteenth century, and Beethoven was one of the first composers to indicate metronome markings in his scores to aid in the performance of his music. After his works were first performed Beethoven added metronome markings, to help musicians of his day perform to his musical expectations. For further exploration, read "Tempo and Character in Beethoven's Music" by Rudolf Kolisch.[2] Once you have a clear understanding of tempo and character markings, observe how those affect melodic themes and motives throughout the work.

Melodic Themes and Motives

> Now I prepare my score much like a conductor, I make a plan. I have a very clear idea of where the composer thinks the most meaningful moments are. I look at the themes and motifs, and where either encounter the most harmonic or rhythmic tension. To look at all four parts simultaneously can be a bit overwhelming, so I try to see where the composer has stashed the theme, or the relics of the theme. It's a bit like a scavenger hunt of musical variations.
> ~ Astrid Schween, cellist, Juilliard String Quartet

It is essential to understand which voice in your ensemble has the melodic theme or motive. Highlighting voices during the performance of a work draws the listeners' attention to the melodic themes or motives. Equally important is to observe how the melody or motive may be passed from one voice to another in the score to bring the listener into the musical conversation. Passing the melody between members of an ensemble creates delightful interplay, like a basketball team passing the ball from one player to the next to score a point.

First, identify melodic themes and motives by highlighting or circling them in the score (see Figure 4.2). In the first movement of Dvořák's String Quartet Op. 96, the

FIGURE 4.2 Melodic lines in Dvořák String Quartet in F Major, Op.96, "The American," Allegro ma non troppo.

score offers a clear picture of the melodic theme, which begins in the viola part and then passes to the first violin.

Next, identify how motives are passed around from voice to voice. One method is to highlight the motive in each voice with a different color. Another method is to mark an arrow where each voice has the motive (see Figure 4.3). Once the melodic themes and motives have been identified in the score, the next step is to identify rhythmic cues.

FIGURE 4.3 Passing the melody in Dvořák String Quartet in F Major, Op.96, "The American," Allegro ma non troppo.

Rhythmic Cues

Marking rhythmic cues is a standard practice in chamber music rehearsal preparation. A *rhythmic cue* is a written indication in the part based on score study which indicates the rhythm of another voice before, during, or after your own line, or silences (*grand pauses*). Marking rhythmic cues in your part enables you to synchronize with the other members of the ensemble and understand how your part fits into the whole. You can develop your own shorthand for indications you write in your part.

We recommend the following steps for marking rhythmic cues into your part:

1. Locate places in the score where the rhythm of another part interconnects with your own.
2. Identify when another voice can help you to come in after a rest, or at the beginning or ending of a phrase.
3. Write the relevant cues into your part (see Figure 4.4).

FIGURE 4.4 Mozart String Quartet in E-flat Major, K. 428, Allegro vivace, cello part.

Identify Rhythmic Partners: Buddy System

In addition to writing in rhythmic cues, it is helpful to write in the name or instrument of the person who plays the same rhythm with you (see Figure 4.5). The Cavani Quartet coined the term *buddy system* as a friendly way to refer to two or more ensemble members playing the same rhythm simultaneously. A *buddy* is a supportive colleague and brings out the joyful nature of chamber music playing.

- ✓ Mark places in the score where you have the same rhythm as another voice.
- ✓ Write rhythmic cues and the name of the instrument (you can use abbreviations) or the name of a colleague in your part.

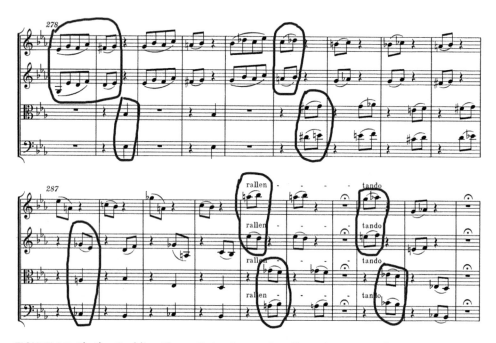

FIGURE 4.5 Rhythm Buddies. Mozart String Quartet in E-flat Major, K. 428, Allegro vivace.

Circle All Silences

Silence is one of the most powerful and dramatic musical devices. Use the score to identify moments of silence within a musical phrase and circle those silences in your own part. These moments of silence can be referred to as a rest or *grand pause*.

First, mark places in the score where all voices have a rest or grand pause together (see Figure 4.6). Next, write them into your part (see Figure 4.7). Figure 4.8 shows the exposition page of the cello part of Mozart String Quartet in E-flat, K. 428, *Allegro Vivace*, illustrating all rhythmic cues.

Score Study   55

FIGURE 4.6 Mozart String Quartet in E-flat Major, K. 428, Allegro vivace, score.

FIGURE 4.7 Mozart String Quartet in E-flat Major, K. 428, Allegro vivace, cello part.

Dynamics

> By assigning personalities to dynamics, it makes the music come alive . . . When you have a four-bar crescendo as opposed to a two-bar crescendo, that changes the emotional content immediately. Particularly with Beethoven, the printed dynamics are not just decibel levels, they have to do with personality and character. The piano has a certain character, and the forte has a certain character.
>
> ~ Earl Carlyss, former member, Juilliard Quartet

Once you have studied melodic themes and motives, and marked rhythmic cues in your part, the next step in score study is to observe the dynamics. The dynamics reveal the character and emotions of a work. The term *dynamics* means "changes in volume in music."[3] *Dynamic markings* are the symbols used by the composer to indicate changes in volume. Beyond indicating volume, the dynamics provide the overall emotional landscape of the work.

The composer's historical context can influence the interpretation of the dynamics. For example, a work by Joseph Haydn written in the eighteenth century may include only a few dynamic markings, while works by Béla Bartók from the twentieth century have detailed dynamic markings.

56 The Art of Collaboration

FIGURE 4.8 Cello part marked up per our score study process. Mozart String Quartet in E-flat Major, K. 428, Allegro vivace, exposition.

Here are a few suggestions to deepen your awareness of the emotional landscape of the work by observing the dynamic markings in the score.

- ✓ Notice the extremes. What are the loudest and softest dynamic markings in the movement?
- ✓ Does the composer mark different dynamics for different instruments simultaneously in a passage?
- ✓ Notice the low and high points, such as beginnings of a *crescendo* or a *diminuendo*. Do these markings happen frequently or sporadically?
- ✓ Look for *subito* dynamics or sudden changes in dynamic contour.
- ✓ Write in the dynamic pacing (tiered dynamics) within a passage, based on the composer's indication of *crescendos* and *diminuendos*. By pacing dynamics, you create musical tension and release (see example of dynamic pacing in Figure 4.9).
  - Begin a *crescendo* with the lowest dynamic and begin a *diminuendo* with the highest dynamic (see Figure 4.9).
  - Write a dynamic for each measure of a *crescendo* or *diminuendo* to ensure a unified approach (see Figure 4.9).
- ✓ Identify all emphasis markings, such as an accent (), *sforzando* (*sfz*), and *fortepiano* (*fp*), which have different functions depending on the composer's

FIGURE 4.9 Example of dynamic pacing. Schubert String Quintet in C Major, Op.163, Allegretto.

58   The Art of Collaboration

context. Approaches to markings which define musical emphasis differ depending on the style and era of music. For further guidance, refer to the chapter on *Techniques for Sound Production*.

Now that you are aware of the dynamics within the work, the next step in score study is to become familiar with harmony and harmonic structure.

Harmony

Different harmonic systems exist around the world and are often the inspiration for a variety of compositions. By understanding the origins of the repertoire that you are performing, you enhance your experience and capability to communicate the music. We encourage you to explore diverse types of scale systems, such as pentatonic scales (Japan and East Asia), Ethiopian Kiñit, Kora scales (West Africa), Gamelan scales (Indonesia), and scales of North India. For more information, read *Musical Scales of the World* by Michael Hewitt.[4]

In this section, we offer a few suggestions on how to begin analyzing diatonic or chromatic harmony which originates from classical Greece. The diatonic scale system is based on *modes*, which date to ancient Greece. The seven *modes*, which include *Ionian, Dorian, Phrygian, Lydian, Mixolydian, Aeolian*, and *Locrian*, are the basis for tonality in Western music. Interesting fact: Dorianne's father was a graduate music student when she was born and she was named after the *Dorian mode.*

One does not need to be a music theory whiz to appreciate and understand harmonic shifts, tension, and resolution. Notice where the harmonies are striking or unusual. In any given phrase of music, there may be moments of tension (dissonance) and release (consonance and cadence), which indicate a sense of push and pull. Harmony also helps you to understand when you can use *rubato*, which can be used to emphasize the tension and release of an important harmonic or melodic moment.

For a deeper understanding of the harmonic structure of a work, expand your music theory knowledge. A multitude of resources are devoted to harmony and harmonic structure.

- ✓ Observe the initial key signature and all key changes within the movement.
- ✓ Notice when the composer uses unison writing to emphasize and dramatize a passage.
- ✓ Notice the intervals in your part, or between the voices within the score. Are they dissonant or consonant?

When you have a dissonant interval, such as a minor second, you will feel a sense of tension between these two notes. The tension resolves when the harmony moves to a consonant interval. The vibrations of the intervals affect you and your listener; you can feel them emotionally and physically. This concept is derived from the *Doctrine of the Affections*, which is a theory of emotions related to painting, music, and theater widely used in the Baroque era based on the work of René Descartes.[5]

Form and Structure

Appreciating the form and structure of a piece of music is like witnessing a magnificent architectural structure. Renowned architect Frank Lloyd Wright viewed buildings as musical structures, "My father taught me to see—to listen—to a symphony as an edifice of sound."[6] Likewise, ensembles may approach a piece of music from the perspective of a system of organized elements that fit together to create a structural whole.

Once you have identified key elements in the score that relate your part to the whole, adopt a bird's-eye view of the work and its compositional structure. Identifying the formal structure of a work informs interpretive decisions about pacing, phrasing, transitions, and tempo relationships which illuminate the shape of a composition. Understanding a work's structure and form allows ensembles to create a meaningful experience for their audience.

The organizational elements that determine the formal structure of a piece of music usually include melody, rhythm, and harmony. In addition, compositional devices such as repetition, variation, and orchestration contribute to the structure.[7] Musical structure is based on the development of these elements.

Form refers to the overall structure of the composition. Among common musical forms in Western classical music scholars refer to this structure as a sectional form, including simple binary (AB), simple ternary (ABA), compound binary (ABAB), rondo, theme and variations, and canonic (e.g., a fugue). These forms may have descriptive names, such as *sonata-allegro*. The sonata is "the most important principle of musical form, or formal type from the classical period well into the twentieth century"[8] and is often the form of the first movement in multi-movement works.

The elements of a *sonata-allegro* movement include introduction, exposition, development, recapitulation, and coda. A brief description of each follows. For a deeper understanding, see Appendix A.

- ✓ **Introduction:** Composers often include an introduction to create a feeling of anticipation for the music that follows. An introduction can be a slow prelude to the faster body of the movement.
- ✓ **Exposition:** The exposition introduces the first and primary theme and a contrasting second theme, which can be more lyrical. A double bar often marks the end of the exposition and beginning of the development.

60 The Art of Collaboration

- ✓ **Development:** The development is an expansion and transformation of the expositional themes through harmonic and rhythmic variation and creative voicing.
- ✓ **Recapitulation:** The recapitulation is announced by the return to the home key and character of the first theme. Composers often save their peak climatic moments for the recapitulation to establish a sense of arrival.
- ✓ **Coda** (In Italian, "tail"): The coda offers a sense of closure and gives the composer an opportunity to summarize the main musical ideas of the movement.

Some compositions do not follow a fixed form and are improvisational (e.g., a fantasia or tone poem). Composer Claude Debussy, wanting to rebel against the traditional *sonata-allegro* form, said the following in in a letter to his publisher in 1907: "I am more and more convinced that music is not, in essence, a thing that can be cast into a traditional and fixed form. It is made up of colors and rhythms."[9] By understanding compositional form, you embark on a musical journey to bring to this experience to life as you play a work.

An Invitation to Play from the Score

Playing from the score allows you to see everyone's part and hear how the parts fit together in real time. With current technology, musicians are now able to perform from the score by using a tablet device, which makes page turns easy. This is an ideal way to learn chamber music. The Borromeo String Quartet often plays from the score by using tablet technology and foot pedals.[10]

Have Fun with Your Score: An Exercise

On the next page, try out your score reading and marking skills on Beethoven's String Quartet Opus 18, number 4 (see Figure 4.10). Have fun studying the score as a group (see Figure 4.11).

- ✓ **Identify the Tempo:** What is the meaning of the words?
- ✓ **Find the Melody:** Decide who has the melody at any given time and mark it.
- ✓ **Circle All Silence:** Mark places in the score where all voices have a rest or *grand pause* together.
- ✓ **Find Rhythm Buddies:** Mark places in the score where you have the same rhythm as one or more instruments at the same time.
- ✓ **Write in Rhythmic Cues:** Find places in the score where other voices have unusual rhythms or subdivisions.
- ✓ **Identify Dynamics:** Find the high and low points of the dynamics. At what level do the crescendos begin? At what level do decrescendos begin?

✓ **Explore Harmony:** For those with a music theory background, find the relationships between the home key signature and new or striking harmonies introduced by the composer. What moods or emotions do the key changes reflect?

FIGURE 4.10 Beethoven String Quartet in c minor, Op.18, No. 4, Allegro ma non tanto.

62 The Art of Collaboration

FIGURE 4.11 Cavani Quartet studying a Beethoven score. (Photo credit: Robert Muller)

5

REHEARSAL PLAYBOOK

> First of all, you need to have a plan, because a plan helps you be intentional about your rehearsals. It does not have to be etched in concrete, it needs to be fluid, it needs to be able to change, but you need to have some plan in mind.
> ~ Dr. Ronald Crutcher, President Emeritus,
> University of Richmond, cellist, Klemperer Trio

In This Chapter:

- Long-Range Plan
- Daily Rehearsal Plan
- Organizing Accountabilities
- Healthy Communication During Rehearsal

This chapter offers suggestions for planning and implementing a constructive and effective rehearsal. This chapter puts a musical spin on the sports playbook approach, offering long-range and daily rehearsal planning guidance. A sports playbook provides practical guidance in areas that directly impact team performance. The concept of a playbook has been adopted in business and organizational settings as a unifying communication tool. Similarly, chamber music ensembles can utilize a rehearsal playbook to promote the group decision-making process, improve time management, and establish overall musical goals. A rehearsal playbook can include a long-range plan with overall musical goals, daily plans for rehearsals, and organizational reminders.

Long-Range Plan

A long-range plan is based on performance goals, such as concerts, coaching sessions, competitions, or community engagement programs. To create a long-range plan, identify rehearsal dates and times by working back from performance goals. The timeframe for the long-range plan is relative to the amount of time available before your performance goal. We suggest creating a written plan specifying the dates and the specific repertoire to be rehearsed on each date. A written plan ensures time is allocated to rehearse all repertoire and that ensemble members know what to prepare for each rehearsal.

For example, a long-range plan for presenting a benefit concert for the local food bank will include dates, times, and locations for each rehearsal, the repertoire of

The Art of Collaboration. Annie Fullard and Dorianne Cotter-Lockard, Oxford University Press. © Oxford University Press 2025.
DOI: 10.1093/oso/9780197673126.003.0006

focus for each rehearsal, and the time allocated for logistics such as coordinating with the food bank staff, publicity, and on-site setup and production.

Daily Rehearsal Plan

> We come to the table prepared. Let's say we've got six pieces to learn. We're clearly not going to work on all of it in one day, so a plan is vital. Have a rehearsal schedule and stick to it as much as you can. Nominate a timekeeper.
> ~ Monica Ellis, bassoonist and founding member of Imani Winds (see Figure 5.1)

In This Section:
- Tuning Routine
- Warmup Routine
- Rehearsing Spots
- Daily Rehearsal Plan Example

The daily rehearsal plan is a part of the chamber music playbook and is related to the long-range plan. The daily plan includes the amount of time allocated for each piece to be rehearsed. This section suggests ideas for an overall rehearsal structure and provides an example for implementing this structure in an hour-long period. Begin with a discussion of the music to rehearse for each session. The recommended overall rehearsal structure could include:

✓ Establish a focused tuning routine at the beginning of each rehearsal.
✓ Warm up together using a scale or Bach chorale.
✓ Play through a movement or a large section of the music.
✓ Each ensemble member chooses "spots" to rehearse.
✓ Play through the movement or section of music again.

FIGURE 5.1 Imani Winds Press Photo. (Photo credit: Shervin Lainez)

Balance rehearsals with a ratio of 60–70 percent playing and 30–40 percent discussion to help ensemble members stay focused, mindful, and adhere to the rehearsal structure.

Tuning Routine

The care with which you tune your instruments sets the atmosphere for the entire rehearsal. Thoughtful tuning tells your subconscious mind it is time to pay attention and listen carefully to each other.

Unify your tuning routine to create a foundation for consistent, improved intonation. Many theories regarding tuning and intonation exist—to read more about tuning, see Stuart Isacoff's book, *Temperament*.[1] For another viewpoint, check out Ross Duffin's book, *How Equal Temperament Ruined Harmony (and Why You Should Care)*.[2] The following steps illustrate a tuning routine for all types of instrumental ensembles.

1. Develop a regular order for each member to tune their instrument. For example, in a string quartet, start with the cello, then viola, second violin, and finally first violin. Follow this order at the beginning of every rehearsal and it will become a more efficient habit.
2. Tune one person at a time while other group members refrain from talking or playing so the person tuning can listen carefully.
3. Use a tuner or a tuning app on a smartphone.
4. Play long, slow tones to adjust to the tuner.

For string ensembles, test each open string together and ensure open strings on all instruments are in tune with each other. Pay careful attention to ensure that open C strings are in tune with open E strings to facilitate resonance and intonation.

Warmup Routine

Create a warmup routine that includes playing scales and Bach chorales together. The warmup routine focuses attention on nonverbal communication and developing a unified ensemble sound. Refer to the chapter on *Techniques for Intonation, Warmup Routine* for detailed guidelines.

Rehearsing Spots

Divide the rehearsal time so each ensemble member has an opportunity to choose "spots" (passages or measures in the music) on which they would like to focus.

66   The Art of Collaboration

This practice facilitates equal participation and enables each member to express their opinions and suggest areas for improvement. Using collaborative rehearsal techniques rather than critiquing for improvement results in a more energized, thoughtful, and fun rehearsal process. Each member facilitates a portion of the rehearsal (5–15 minutes per person). It is helpful to use a timer.

Daily Rehearsal Plan Example

In Table 5.1, a 1-hour string quartet rehearsal is broken down into activities (tuning routine, warmup, playing through a movement or section, and spots), with time allocated for each. This example can be modified for any type of ensemble, expanded for longer rehearsals, and spots can be facilitated by members in any order. Appendix C contains a rehearsal plan summary that can be used as quick reference during rehearsals.

Table 5.1 Example plan: String quartet within a typical hour-long rehearsal (approximate timing).

Approximate Time	Activity
5 minutes	Tuning routine: Each member tunes individually with a tuner and tests each string as a group.
5 minutes	Warmup routine: Play a Bach Chorale, scales together, or a group improvisation.
5–10 minutes	Play through a movement or a section that will be the focus of this rehearsal.
10 minutes	Spots: Cellist leads rehearsal spots by choosing the tempos with the metronome, discussing tempo characters, and asking the group to try a section of the music faster and slower in relation to the marked tempo. Group uses *Chamber Music Aerobics* for rhythmic alignment (Chapter 9) and writes decisions in the parts.
10 minutes	Spots: Violist leads rehearsal spots by choosing to work on one section for listening, sound, and intonation and playing through it slowly, identifying all the perfect intervals. Group uses *Techniques for Intonation* for tonal color and resonance (Chapter 10) and writes decisions in the parts.
10 minutes	Spots: Second violinist leads rehearsal spots by saying, "I like where this is going!" They find sections for pacing *rubato* and listening for small subdivisions. Group uses *Techniques for Strategic Listening and Balance* (Chapter 13) and writes decisions in the parts.
10 minutes	Spots: First violinist leads rehearsal spots by asking the group to focus on dynamic character to add nuance and inflection by emphasizing harmonic changes and balancing the lines. Group uses *LBAD* (*Live, Breathe, and Die*) (Chapter 14) to understand colleagues' interpretations of the passage and relate the first violin part to the other parts. Group writes decisions in the parts.
5–10 minutes	Play through the movement or several sections again to reinforce the decisions made during the rehearsal.

Organizing Accountabilities

Organizing accountabilities is the process of defining the "jobs" for each member of the ensemble. Organize your individual accountabilities so that everyone shares responsibility for the ensemble's progress. Each member takes on "jobs" or roles in the group—one or more responsibilities to support the group which promotes an equal balance of management between members and facilitates important logistics, such as finding adequate rehearsal space, or acquiring music. We recommend you consider the job roles described in Table 5.2. Whether you are a professional,

Table 5.2 Organizing roles for ensemble members.

Role/Responsibility	Description
For All Types of Ensembles	
Rehearsal logistics coordinator	Reserve rehearsal space, ensuring chairs are available, sending schedule reminders, etc.
Librarian	A group member can be responsible for obtaining editions of works and obtaining works by living composers.
Communication liaison	Person who responds to email, text, and phone communications related to group activities.
For Student and Amateur Ensembles	
Liaison with chamber music coach	Schedule coaching sessions and discuss repertoire with coach
For Emerging and Professional Ensembles	
Marketing and social media coordinator	Maintains online presence through various social media channels.
Financial manager	Manages bank accounts and taxes, if applicable.
Grant writer	Researches grant opportunities, writes grant applications, follows up on grant submissions and reports.
Development and fundraising coordinator	Develops relationships with funding organizations and donors.
Community engagement and education coordinator.	Develops relationships with community organizations, such as local businesses, restaurants, art galleries, bookstores, and schools.
Liaison with arts presenters	Develops and maintains relationships with chamber music series and presenters.
Liaison with composers and guest artists	Communicates with collaborative guest artists and composers.
Residency coordinator	Organizes and coordinates residency activities with sponsoring presenters and institutions.
Liaison with professional management	Communicates with manager on artistic and logistic decisions.

68 The Art of Collaboration

emerging, amateur, or student group, attention to organizing accountabilities is a key to sustaining a successful, positive chamber music experience.

Once the ensemble has established jobs or responsibilities for each member it is advisable to have a system in place for reporting on finished items and addressing upcoming tasks that contribute to the group. Set up short meetings apart from your rehearsal time. Keep the meetings efficient by giving every member a chance to speak briefly about past items and upcoming items that affect the quartet. Take notes to maintain a list of upcoming tasks shared with the group.

Hyeyung Sol Yoon, violinist of the Del Sol Quartet and former member of the Chiara Quartet offered us a technique for meetings at the beginning of rehearsal. She explained that the Chiara Quartet began their rehearsals by reporting on their respective activities on behalf of the quartet. This system helped them avoid conflict because they all agreed on the process, and in turn they created a forum for dialogue and a more positive working environment. Knowing they had a system and forum to discuss and resolve issues helped the Chiara Quartet to navigate rehearsals with an attitude of openness. Hyeyung Sol Yoon describes their process in detail (Box 5.1):

Box 5.1 Process for Group Accountabilities

Hyeyung Sol Yoon, violinist, Del Sol String Quartet explains the Chiara Quartet process for group accountabilities:

We needed to come up with a system to rehearse with each other, that protected our boundaries, and provided a bit more structure, so we could be more open to each other. We came up with this system of doing stand-up meetings at the beginning of rehearsals, where we would stand in a circle and ask each other three questions. We then took turns answering these questions. After this process we began our rehearsal.

1. What did you do in relation to quartet rehearsal or on behalf of the quartet since our last rehearsal?
   Answers could be as simple as "I practiced this difficult part," or "I emailed this person." It could be business-related or musical, and a way to align everyone on the same wavelength.
2. What got in the way of doing quartet work?
   Answers could be as simple as, "Well, I was not feeling well yesterday, so I had to postpone doing this," or "In the last rehearsal, I felt something was said that affected me in a negative way, and I would like to resolve that." We created a safe space to talk about what prevented us from doing something productive for the quartet.
3. What are we going to do today?
   This is the moment when everyone talks about what their priorities are for that rehearsal. This really worked for us.

Healthy Communication During Rehearsal

> You say what needs to be said, in a nice tone and a sense of absolute trust that they [your colleagues] can achieve anything that you ask them to do.
>
> ~ Peter Oundjian, former member, Tokyo String Quartet

This section offers tips for healthy dialogue and communication during rehearsals. *How* you say something during rehearsal is just as important as *what* you say. Taking the time to consider the impact of your words and how your colleagues might respond is integral to productive and successful rehearsals. See the chapter "Working Well Together" for detailed guidance.

In This Section:
• Using Focus Words or Phrases
• Positive Communication While Rehearsing Spots
• Rehearsal Advice from Earl Carlyss

Using Focus Words or Phrases

Before playing through a movement or section, each member can share a focus word or phrase related to the musical interpretation, ensemble technique, or another performance aspect. This activity will help the group set an intention before playing. Choose a word or phrase that will inspire your colleagues.

Some examples are as follows: (1) *communication*, which might imply looking up once per measure; (2) *balance*, which implies listening to the melodies throughout the passage; (3) *exaggerate the dynamics*, which could imply increasing the range of volume; (4) *bring out the characters*, which could mean emphasizing the character or emotional quality of the music; and (5) *cue together*, implying greater physical movement and visual connection.

Positive Communication While Rehearsing Spots

Listening carefully to your colleagues is as important as adding your opinion to a dialogue. Guidance is included in leading spots and responding to suggestions from colleagues.

When you are leading spots, use phrases to invite your colleagues, such as "Could we try this?" or "How about trying this here?" In addition, use phrases that address the group rather than an individual, such as, "Could we work on intonation here and build up chords slowly from the bass?" Approach the work by inspiring and inviting your colleagues to participate rather than demanding they try something.

70   The Art of Collaboration

When responding to a suggestion, use "Yes, and . . ." and immediately try the idea as if it were your own. Once you have tried an idea, ask your colleague if you have demonstrated it. Dialogue may follow, leading to another way of approaching or reframing the idea. Through this exchange, you will learn something new and engage in true collaboration, increasing the potential for improvement and change. Chapter 2, "Working Well Together," includes many ideas to create healthy dialogue and adopting a "Yes, and . . ." approach.

The Cavani Quartet was fortunate to work closely during their formative years with Earl Carlyss, former second violinist of the Juilliard Quartet, at the Center for Advanced Quartet Studies at the Aspen Music Festival. Mr. Carlyss related wonderful anecdotes, stories, and valuable advice. We now share some of his wisdom (Box 5.2).

Box 5.2 Rehearsal Advice from Earl Carlyss

✓ Begin with a good attitude.

✓ Read through the movement. Read it more than once without comment to let the music talk to you. It will tell you what it wants you to do if you listen. Start with that approach.

✓ Now you know how the music sounds. Next, determine the character of the music. What is the composer trying to tell us with this music?

✓ Cover large sections, such as from the beginning to the exposition. For example, you can talk about the differences between the first and second themes in terms of character. What is the character of each theme?

✓ The most important thing is not to get bogged down in technical details early on. As you become more familiar with the piece, the technical things will fall into alignment automatically.

This chapter includes foundational elements to aid ensembles in developing their unique rehearsal playbook. Ensembles who establish a healthy balance between organizational activities and creative work are able to sustain positive relationships among group members. A group that works well together, plays well together.

PART III

INSPIRATION AND INTERPRETATION

The whole rehearsal process is designed around how do you make something worth hearing? Any memorable performance is memorable because of specific events that are interesting and finely crafted and focused, such as character and timing. That's creating memorable moments.

~ Norman Fischer, Cellist, Shepherd School of Music,
Head of Chamber Music, Tanglewood Music Center,
Former Member of Concord String Quartet

In Part III:

Chapter 6: Exploring the Character
Chapter 7: Exploring the Composer's World

As musicians, we aspire to create a living musical landscape to share—with each other and our listeners—bringing the music to life through interpretation. Part III guides your ensemble through the interpretive process of defining character, moods, emotions, and meaning by illuminating approaches for researching composers and the context of their works. It concludes with one of the most vital aspects of learning and performing chamber music: collaborating with living composers. The future of chamber music depends on actively commissioning works and working with composers to expand the repertoire.

6

EXPLORING THE CHARACTER

I studied with John Celentano at the Eastman School of Music. One great idea he taught us was to sight-read a new piece at each lesson. He demanded that we play with all the dynamics and expression as we sight-read, right from the start. You could miss the notes, but you needed to get the character right from the start. That has stayed with me.

~ Peter Salaff, former member, Cleveland String Quartet

In This Chapter:

- Interpreting Moods, Emotions, and Meaning
- Finding Your Tonal Color Palette
- Engaging Your Imagination
- Storytelling
- Drawing on Inspiration from Around the World

Deepening our understanding of musical meaning and character lies at the heart of the rehearsal process. The character of the music is the essence of what you wish to communicate as an ensemble. We included this chapter to emphasize the importance of establishing musical character as a focal point of the rehearsal process.

Around the world, music in every culture expresses our deepest emotions and celebrates our greatest triumphs. This intrinsic need to use a medium for expression has existed for centuries—human beings created the first musical instrument more than 40,000 years ago, a Paleolithic flute made of mammoth tusk and bird bone.[1] Artists across all disciplines have written about the power of music to move us and deepen our understanding of each other without words.

We encourage ensemble members to discuss the character, mood, and emotions of the music before making technical decisions. An abundance of references, articles, and program notes can be found through research on the internet. Dialogue about character and musical meaning leads to a diversity of ideas and deeper insights. Working together, you can create a more powerful interpretation.

Interpreting Moods, Emotions, and Meaning

Music conveys an extraordinary variety of moods, emotions, and meanings. The joy of communicating emotion and meaning to each other and your audience is one of

The Art of Collaboration. Annie Fullard and Dorianne Cotter-Lockard, Oxford University Press. © Oxford University Press 2025.
DOI: 10.1093/oso/9780197673126.003.0007

74 The Art of Collaboration

In This Section:

- Descriptive Words
- Historical References
- Singing or Dancing?

the most profound experiences we share as performing artists. Alain de Botton and John Armstrong, authors of *Art as Therapy*, share: "It lies in the power of art to honour the elusive but real value of ordinary life. It can teach us to be more just to ourselves as we endeavor to make the best of our circumstances. Art can do the opposite of glamourizing the unattainable; it can reawaken us to the genuine merit of life as we are forced to lead it."[2]

As chamber musicians, the discovery and communication of meaning can transform and bond your ensemble. Here are some suggestions for discovering moods, emotions, and meaning during the rehearsal process:

- ✓ Play a passage of the music. Discuss characters, moods, emotions, and meaning. Be open to ideas that differ from your own and try them in a fully committed way. Find common ground.
- ✓ Write down key descriptive words in your music.
- ✓ Allow yourself to have an intuitive emotional reaction in the moment. How does the passage make you feel when you play it? How do you react to the musical language: for example; harmony, tempo, texture, and dynamics?
- ✓ What do you think the composer intended us to feel as performers and listeners?
- ✓ Based on your research about the composer, what do you think the composer may have felt while they wrote the piece or passage?

Descriptive Words

You're not limiting yourself to plain notation, you're creating something that would have some shape or some motion or being a little more human. [I said to my students], "The image that I'm getting when I'm looking at this notation is that it should sound like bird wings flapping." It turns out when they saw the composer in Denmark, he explained, "I'm thinking about birds flapping."

~ Norman Fischer, cellist, Shepherd School of Music,
Head of Chamber Music, Tanglewood Music Center,
former member of Concord String Quartet

Applying descriptive words such as adjectives or focus words helps to evoke character and develop a unified approach to the emotional meaning represented in the music. For example, the opening phrase of the Mozart Quartet K. 387 in G major creates a welcoming and positive mood (see Figure 6.1). One can translate the optimism of this passage into descriptive phrases such as *bright blue sky* or *warm greeting*. Once you write these into your part, consider how these descriptors might affect your technical approach. In this extraordinary passage, Mozart also changes dynamics abruptly from *forte* to *piano* in alternate bars, which may suggest an alternation between an outgoing and shy personality, rather than loud and soft.

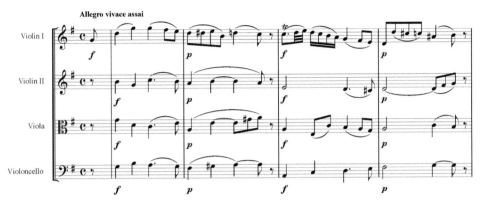

FIGURE 6.1 Mozart String Quartet in G Major, K. 387, Allegro vivace assai.

Violist and pedagogue Karen Tuttle created a teaching tool with a list of descriptive words based on the five basic emotions of love, joy, anger, fear, and sorrow.[3] Our beloved colleague, violinist Joseph Kromholz, along with the students at the Encore Chamber Music Institute String Quartet Intensive, helped us develop and organize a comprehensive list that can help you find a descriptive word to fit a particular passage. This list is included in Appendix B.

Historical References

Research historical accounts of live performances created by contemporaries of composers to better understand the context of a work. For example, while researching Beethoven's string quartets, Annie received a reference from the Borromeo Quartet to an article by pianist and former student of Beethoven, Carl Czerny. Czerny documented his observations of Beethoven's live performances by using descriptive words to capture the variety of characters in the music.[4]

We refer to this list during our rehearsals and when we teach because it exemplifies the range of characters expressed in a single Beethoven performance. Annie carries this list around in her violin case for extra inspiration! The following is translated from the original German and adapted from the original text (Box 6.1).

> **Box 6.1 Carl Czerny's list of descriptive words**
>
> Unruly, serious, tragic, teasing, weighty, fantastic, humorous, pathetic, lulling, firm, intimate, bewitching, determined, fleeting, complaining, religious, brilliant, joyous, strong, roaring, singing, pious, noisy, peaceful, capricious, tender, lively, touching, chorale-like, witty, light, gentle, delicate, good-natured, charming, jocose, dramatic, powerful, virile, flattering, exalted, sparkling, marked, dejected, simple, melancholy, speaking, elegant, graceful, merry, profound, resolute, serene, naive, dreamy, lofty, heroic, unaffected, sensitive.

Singing or Dancing?

> We would sing for each other. We would play for each other.
> ~ Paul Katz, former member, Cleveland String Quartet,
> founder CelloBello

Your ensemble can explore character and meaning by asking: "Is the music singing or dancing?" Dance is intrinsic to the human spirit and our need to express ourselves through movement. Our ability to create vocal qualities (i.e., sing) with our instruments is also essential to the pursuit of expression. As a starting point in the interpretive process, these two modes of expression can be catalysts for interpreting character.

Exploring music's singing or dancing qualities can lift the notes off the page through motion and movement, freeing your interpretive process. If the music feels static or bogged down as you play, imagine it as a dance to boost group energy, which can lead to smiles all around. Approaching music as singing also enables you to find natural moments to breathe. This process can guide choices for timing, inflection, and phrasing. The chapters "Sound Production" and "Projecting Expression" offer guidance in applying vocal techniques and choosing vocalists to inspire your interpretation.

Finding Your Tonal Color Palette

> It's not enough to have a nice sound. You need to have what I call a kaleidoscopic sound. If you are a painter and you only have 10 colors on your palette, it's going to be limited in what you can do with it. But if you have 200 colors on your palette, you can do a lot more.
> ~ Earl Carlyss, former member, Juilliard String Quartet

A compelling ensemble sound is filled with nuance, color, and meaning based on an interpretation of the score. In this section, we offer two ways to ignite the imagination and enhance a group's conception of tonal color. First, visual art can aid the interpretive process by imagining the sound as a color within a musical composition. Second, as instrumentalists, it is beneficial to emulate singers and dancers to produce a vocal quality and movement in our playing.

Visual art can be used as an interpretive tool. It is wonderful to receive inspiration from visual artists in relation to instrumental sound production. Painters use a variety of brushstrokes, colors, and mediums to create magical worlds in a two-dimensional field. As musicians, we can create paintings with sound.

Neurologist-physician Oliver Sacks presented the idea of the intersection between visual and aural senses by exploring a phenomenon called synesthesia. In his book

Musicophilia Sacks described how visual, audio, or other sense signals can be "cross-activated" by the brain into simultaneous sense experiences.[5] Some people literally see colors when they hear different musical tones.

According to Sacks, "musical synesthesia—especially color effects experienced while listening to or thinking of music is one of the most common, and perhaps the most dramatic."[6] Sacks tells the story of American composer Michael Torke, who has associated colors with different musical keys since he was young. Torke says the color associations have been constant in relation to different keys, and the colors "appear spontaneously" when he hears scales, arpeggios, and music written in a particular key. You can find recordings of Torke's Color Music on YouTube, or visit Torke's website for further information on his Color Pieces. This is an intriguing example of how the intersection between visual and aural senses inspired a musician to compose music.

Hear the Color (Ode to Oliver Sacks)

> Music is the expression of the movement of the waters, the play of curves described by changing breezes.
>
> ~ Claude Debussy

We encourage you to explore sensory convergence (in this case, relate visual to aural senses) as an interpretive tool. Research the visual art (paintings, architecture, sculpture) created during the same era as the composer of your repertoire.

- ✓ Explore works that reflect the energy, color, and texture of the music you are playing.
- ✓ Examine the brush strokes in the painting, or the surface texture of the sculpture, or the scope of the architecture.
- ✓ Imagine how the artist used their tools to create, and then translate it to create a variety of articulations with your instrument.

As an example, we chose two paintings which represent the sound world of Ravel and Debussy. Two of our favorite string quartets composed by Maurice Ravel and Claude Debussy invite us to link the music to the visual art created during the late nineteenth to the early twentieth century.

We can compare different types of paintbrush strokes to a variety of articulations. For instance, in the second movement of the Ravel String Quartet, we imagine the pointillism and lively quality of George Seurat in the pizzicato texture in Figures 6.2 and 6.3.

In the second example, we relate the slow movement of the Debussy String Quartet to the unfathomable beauty of Monet's series of Water Lily paintings in Figures 6.4 and 6.5. Annie relates her personal experience:

FIGURE 6.2 Ravel String Quartet in F Major, Assez vif-très rhythmé, 1903.

FIGURE 6.3 George Seurat, "La Senna alla Grande-Jatte," 1888.

FIGURE 6.4 Debussy String Quartet in g minor, Op.10, Andantino, doucement expressif, 1893.

FIGURE 6.5 "Le Bassin aux Nymphéas," Claude Monet, 1899.

When I play the slow movement of the Debussy quartet, I visualize the tranquility, mystery, and melancholy of Monet's Water Lily paintings. I translate those characters to colors created through a variety of techniques. I experience a response to the sublime and moving harmony, and the ebb and flow of the music, which remind me of the water and the dapples of light through the trees. I constantly adapt my sound through the bow contact point, speed, and pressure. I adapt my *vibrato* speed and width as well, to synchronize with colleagues and communicate the profound beauty of the music to the audience.

Music can also inspire the creation of visual art. The Cavani Quartet offers a program called Music, Art, and Poetry (MAP) for school-age students. The MAP program is designed to provide the opportunity for children to interpret music through visual art and poetry with the goals to give every child the opportunity to create art through musical inspiration, promote the power of art as a form of self-expression and a way to relate to the world, foster each child's independent thought and self-esteem through interpretation and performance, and to foster community by creating a joyful and moving collaborative performance. Figure 6.6 is an example of a student's visual art interpretation of the slow movement of Debussy's String Quartet.

In addition to your own research, we encourage you to visit your local art museum, galleries, or any contemporary art exhibit to expand your exposure to visual art. Furthermore, we invite you to walk around community neighborhoods to observe architectural features and street art that strike you as intriguing.

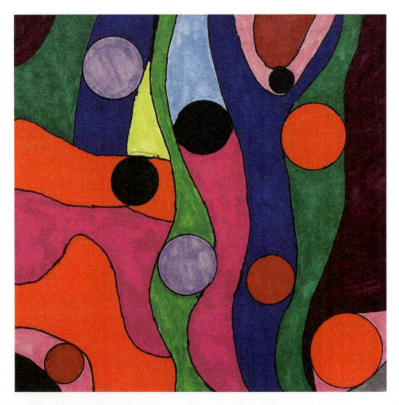

FIGURE 6.6 Artwork Inspired by Debussy, Ruffing Montessori School, guided by art specialist Kate Bennett, art by Lee Haremza, middle school.

Engaging Your Imagination

Visualizing images while one plays is a powerful tool for interpretation. The brain translates images into emotions which are expressed as we play. When you focus on an image in your mind's eye, the brain enables you to transmit meaning, emotions, and the character of the music to your listeners.

- ✓ As you interpret sections of the music, agree on an image or scene for each section.
- ✓ Draw or paint a mental picture while you play. You can even use colored pens or watercolors to create these images on paper.
- ✓ Imagine a dance to a passage or movement. How would you choreograph it?
- ✓ Write a story as a group about the music, which expresses various characters and atmospheres. This is a great team building exercise to design characters based on melodies or motives.

Storytelling

For thousands of years in every culture around the world, people have used music to communicate stories—some with spiritual meaning; some for rituals and rites of passage; some to celebrate or commemorate life events, marriages, or funerals; and some related to war and peace. These musical stories became part of folklore and served to pass history down through generations. This process continues today.

As you become familiar with your repertoire (the foundational components of the piece), take the time to understand the deeper stories or imagery that may be a part of the composer's language. Many composers, including Beethoven, Mendelssohn, Schubert, Tchaikovsky, Prokofiev, Sibelius, and Ravel, often used their music as a personal diary, expressing life's great joys and triumphs as well as profound grief, sorrow, and suffering. For Bartók and Ginastera, their work reflects and responds to the ancient, rich, and vivid folk music tradition of their own culture from Eastern Europe and North Africa (Bartók) and Latin America (Ginastera). For Czechoslovakian composer Bedřich Smetana, he titled his String Quartet No. 1 (1876) "Z mého života"—"From my life." It was to be his dramatic confession, a work depicting the course of his life, "using four instruments speaking among themselves in something like a friendly circle."[7]

The Cavani Quartet performs a work inspired by a poem, *Breakfast at the Ibis*, written by Mwatabu S. Okantah, Professor and Poet in Residence in the Department of Pan-African Studies at Kent State University, Ohio.[8] This musical version of storytelling is inspired by the African cultural tradition of passing stories of daily life from one generation to the next. In the poem, Professor Okantah describes his experience and observations while waiting in line to eat at a restaurant in London (see Figure 6.7).

82 The Art of Collaboration

FIGURE 6.7 Mwatabu Okantah and Cavani Quartet. (Photo credit: Amina Okantah)

The music, composed by Merry Peckham, is for narrator, string quartet, and West African talking drum (dundun, see Figure 6.8), whose pitch can be regulated to mimic the tone and prosody of human speech.[9] The string players use special effects (*col legno*, *glissando*, *pizzicato*, humming while playing) to create a magical sound world that depicts the atmosphere of the poem.

FIGURE 6.8 West African dundun. (Image by Albrecht Fietz from Pixabay)

As performers contemplate and comprehend the deeper meaning behind the music, ambiguities of interpretation become clearer. We recommend staying curious about musical traditions outside your own—the joy of discovery is unlimited, which may even resonate with your own story.

Drawing Inspiration from Around the World

On every continent and in every culture, we can discover a unique musical language and history through music. Many references in this book originate from the Western musical tradition. However, it is vital to note that many composers draw their inspiration from sources around the world in addition to their place of origin. A wonderful resource for information about world rhythms and harmonic systems is *Planet Musician: The World Music Sourcebook for Musicians* by Julie Lyonn Lieberman.[10] You can also find resources from the series *Rough Guides to World Music.*[11]

As musical artists, we possess the ability to communicate and understand human nature in a unique way. When we translate the human condition into musical meaning, it allows us to connect and be understood. Interpreting character, emotion, mood, and meaning through music is fundamental to our existence.

7

EXPLORING THE COMPOSER'S WORLD

> I encourage students to read about the life of the composer, to familiarize themselves with the time-period and to listen to other works by the composer. Listen to the songs of Schubert and Mendelssohn, listen to the words of the songs, and think about what they mean. When you are rehearsing the music, I suggest students put words to the music. Tell a story.
>
> ~ Peter Salaff, former member, Cleveland String Quartet

In This Chapter:

- Investigating the Era
- Exploring the Composer's Voice
- Collaborating with Living Composers

This chapter offers suggestions for researching the composer to ignite the interpretive process. We provide guidance on collaboration with living composers, and present a rehearsal technique to inspire your inner composer through improvisation.

In addition to score study and analysis, it is equally beneficial to understand the historical context and life experiences influencing the composer's creative process. Imagine conversing with a composer of a prior era and approaching them as if they were contemporaries, treating them with respect and reverence. If you are interpreting the works of living composers, take every opportunity to work together in real-time.

This chapter also offers a choreographed journey of discovery through the composers' influences and inspirations, social and political context, and how they reacted to the world around them through the creative process. Finally, it revisits working together with living composers, as this experience will enrich your understanding of the works written in the past. Throughout this chapter, be curious, and enjoy the process of deepening your knowledge and empowering a more convincing interpretation.

Investigating the Era: Trends and Styles

Artists are often influenced by societal trends and styles. Understanding the effect of these trends and styles on the composer offers a more nuanced understanding of their motivation. Knowledge about a composer's language, cultural heritage, and

The Art of Collaboration. Annie Fullard and Dorianne Cotter-Lockard, Oxford University Press. © Oxford University Press 2025. DOI: 10.1093/oso/9780197673126.003.0008

spiritual beliefs can deepen the interpretive process, opening the mind to expansive ideas, experiences, and perspectives. Moreover, it is fun to discover compositional influences based on art, architecture, and social trends in fashion and cuisine.

> **In This Section:**
>
> - Art and Architecture
> - Literature
> - The Natural World

Our perspectives and worldviews are shaped by events that occur during the era in which we live. Current events influence artists of all genres, many of whom express emotions through their art in response to trauma and joy. For example, Picasso's masterpiece *Guernica* depicts the torture and misery of war, influenced by the rise of Nazi Germany and Fascist Italy prior to the Second World War. Similarly, Shostakovich wrote his eighth string quartet in 1960 in memory of the victims of fascism and war and related to his personal experiences living through that era. Gabriela Lena Frank wrote her rhapsodically joyful string quartet *Leyendas: A Peruvian Walkabout* (2001) by drawing on her exploration of Peruvian folk music and instruments, while Felix Mendelssohn wrote the String Quartet Opus 13 in a minor to depict a love poem he wrote.

Here are a few suggestions to enhance your interpretive process by understanding the historical and social context of a composer's work:

- ✓ Research events in and around the era in which the composer wrote music: What world events, life experiences, or impactful relationships may have influenced their musical creativity?
- ✓ Read a biography of the composer and research biographical notes about the specific work under study.
- ✓ Examine trends and styles of the era: What were the social scene, norms, and culture like during their life?
- ✓ Explore literature of the era for sources of inspiration and other contextual elements.

Viewing Art and Architecture

Spend time observing visual art and architecture created during the composer's life. Are there similarities or comparisons that would translate into interpretive decisions? For example, looking at ornate and opulent Baroque architecture and paintings can evoke similar emotional associations with the music of composers such as Vivaldi, Corelli, and Bach.

In addition, assess whether the visual art of the period reflects the music's character. One of the most breathtaking painting movements—now referred to as Impressionism—concurrently evolved while Debussy composed his music. While Debussy did not like the term *impressionism* to describe his music, he used distinct harmonic coloration of the primary motive throughout his String Quartet in G,

Opus 10 in the same way painters such as Monet, Seurat, Renoir, and Pissarro used brush strokes and a color palette to represent natural light and shadow.

Like Debussy's use of diverse harmony to express the same motive through a work, Monet painted a series of twenty-eight paintings to capture the light at different times of the day and year on the same Cathedral in Rouen, France (Box 7.1). You can explore these in a blog by Dan Scott called "How Claude Monet Documented Light Using the Rouen Cathedral."[1]

> **Box 7.1 Listening Exercise**
>
> Listen to the first movement of Debussy's String Quartet while observing images of Monet's Rouen Cathedral paintings. Notice how the opening motive returns repeatedly with a different harmonization. Imagine each harmony as a different hue and compare the color you identified with the colors of Monet's paintings of the cathedral at various times of the day. By engaging in this process with your ensemble, you can have wonderful discussions about the musical score in relation to visual art.

As an example of artists influencing and responding to each other's work, Aristide Maillol created a sculptural response to the music of Debussy to mirror his aesthetic break from the heavy emotional drama of German romanticism of the nineteenth century (see Figure 7.1). Debussy focused on the subtleties of color and light, using a different tonal language based on the pentatonic scale and traditional East Asian music. Maillol created a graceful female form, bending forward, unhindered by arms or a head, focusing on the simplicity and beauty of the human body.

FIGURE 7.1 "Monumentà Claude Debussy" by Aristide Maillol (Photo taken by D. Cotter-Lockard, at Musée d'art Hyacinthe Rigaud, Perpignan)

Exploring Literature

Literature of the composer's era may offer insight into the context in which artists live and create their works. Many composers were, and continue to be, inspired by poets and writers of their time. For example, Leoš Janáček wrote a string quartet called *The Kreutzer Sonata*, inspired by Leo Tolstoy's novella of the same name, and twentieth-century pianist/composer Andre Previn created a suite of four songs in 1994 based on the poetry of Toni Morrison and written for cello, piano, and a soprano singer.

At the dawn of Romanticism, composers including Beethoven, Mendelssohn, and Schuman collaborated with poets such as Goethe, Heine, and Novalis to create the *Art Song* or *Lieder*. Another connection between composer and poet occurred in the early nineteenth century when Beethoven adapted Friedrich Schiller's poem titled "An die Freunde" (Ode to Joy) in the final movement of the 9th Symphony as a call for freedom, equality, and humanity.

Observing the Natural World

Composers frequently draw inspiration from the natural world. This section highlights a few who express a readily apparent and dramatic relationship with the natural world.

Debussy drew from and named several compositions inspired by nature. Some of his most profound and famous works include the symphonic tone poem *La Mer* (The Sea) and *Clair de Lune* (Moonlight), the latter of which is a movement from the *Suite Bergamasque* for piano. When interpreting Debussy's chamber music, one can apply the same relationship to the natural world, playing passages by expressing the ebb and flow of waves or wind. Debussy describes this phenomenon: "There is nothing more musical than a sunset. He who feels what he sees will find no more beautiful example of development in all that book which, alas, musicians read but too little—the book of Nature."

Hungarian composer and ethnomusicologist Béla Bartók also found nature to be a creative force illuminating our humanity. In his published memoirs, Bartók's son writes that his father "loved nature in all its manifestations."[2] Bartók recognized and interpreted the natural world through "night music" incorporating instrumental techniques imitating the sounds of insects, birds, and the hum of evenings in the woods or under the stars.[3] He held that the symmetry and asymmetry of nature were as beautiful as any great work of art and that nature was the inspiration for folk music, which he incorporated into his compositions. Bartók's relationship

88 The Art of Collaboration

with nature offers a more profound perspective for performers and interpreters of his music.

Exploring the Composer's Voice

> I think that sometimes, particularly with Beethoven quartets, I can almost sense his presence. It's a strange thing to say, but I can feel him somehow. Particularly with the late quartets. . . . A presence, of the composer being there.
>
> ~ Peter Salaff, former member, Cleveland String Quartet

In This Section:

- Researching Life Events
- Listening to Other Works
- Letters and Quotes

The composer lives in a context, which in turn affects the way they experience the world and express themselves through music. This section offers approaches to deepen your understanding of the context which informs the composer's worldview and voice.

Researching Life Events

Composers are often motivated to create works based on their life experiences and impactful relationships. Exploring these relationships can lead to a thorough interpretation, which reveals insight into the composer's creative process. Begin with a good biography of the composer and see where the journey takes you.

An example of an impactful relationship of mutual inspiration is composer Antonin Dvořák's fortuitous meeting with singer Harry T. Burleigh (1866–1949). Dvořák moved to the United States to become Director of the National Conservatory of Music. Burleigh received his early musical training in Erie, Pennsylvania, and subsequently came to New York City as a scholarship student at the National Conservatory at age twenty-six. Burleigh was an accomplished all-around musician with a fine baritone voice. He played double bass and timpani in the Conservatory Orchestra and later taught *solfège* and piano. Burleigh introduced Dvořák to "plantation songs" (spirituals) that he learned from his blind, formerly enslaved grandfather. Dvořák encouraged Burleigh to write, publish, and perform these songs. Burleigh described these songs as "practically the only music in America which meets the scientific definition of Folk Song."[4] For his part, Dvořák steeped himself in these melodies and used them in his American works, including his *Symphony from the New World* and Quartet Opus 96, *The American.*

Burleigh became Dvořák's colleague and family friend. Burleigh remained in New York teaching voice, where he gave annual performances at St. George's

Exploring the Composer's World **89**

Episcopal Church and Temple Emanu-El. He also frequently toured the United States and Europe.

Listening to Other Works by the Composer

Broaden your perspective by listening to works by the same composer, including music they have written for multiple genres, including ballets, operas, film scores, symphonies, sonatas, and other chamber music. For example, Russian composers Prokofiev and Shostakovich wrote ballet, film, and opera music with themes and motivic gestures directly related to those in their chamber music. The rhythmic intensity in Prokofiev's music for the ballet *Romeo and Juliet* helps visualize the characters in his string quartets. The use of Shostakovich's initials as a musical motive is evident in the 8th String Quartet and the cello concerto.

Reading Letters and Quotes

Research and read letters and quotes in the composer's words to better understand their voice. These words illustrate their personality and the context in which they created their works.

One of the most prominent sources for understanding Beethoven and the struggles he endured is the *Heiligenstadt Testament*—a passionate and intensely personal letter written by Beethoven to his brothers, explaining his sense of hopelessness to communicate while his hearing deteriorated. It offers a window into his inner life and emotions and his heroic commitment to art as a healing life force. A few years after Beethoven wrote the *Heiligenstadt Testament*, he composed three quartets dedicated to Count Razumovsky. The slow movements of Op. 59 No. 1 and No. 2 express Beethoven's emotional landscape. These movements convey not only his depth of despair, but also his sense of hope and responsibility to fulfill his artistic destiny. Included here is an English translation by Barry Cooper (Box 7.2).[5]

Box 7.2 For My Brothers Carl and [Johann] Beethoven

O you men who think or say I am hostile, peevish, or misanthropic, how greatly you wrong me. You do not know the secret cause which makes me seem so to you. From childhood on, my heart and soul were full of the tender feeling of goodwill, and I was always inclined to accomplish great deeds. But just think, for six years now I have had an incurable condition, made worse by incompetent doctors, from year to year deceived with hopes of getting better, finally forced to face the prospect of a lasting infirmity (whose cure will perhaps take years or even be impossible). Though born with a fiery, lively temperament, susceptible to the diversions of society, I soon had to withdraw myself, to spend my life alone. And if I wished

90 The Art of Collaboration

at times to ignore all this, oh how harshly was I pushed back by the doubly sad experience of my bad hearing; and yet it was impossible for me to say to people, "Speak louder, shout, for I am deaf." Ah, how could I possibly admit weakness of the *one sense* which should be more perfect in me than in others, a sense which I once possessed in the greatest perfection, a perfection such as few in my profession have or ever have had.

Oh I cannot do it; so forgive me if you see me draw back when I would gladly have mingled with you. My misfortune is doubly painful to me as I am bound to be misunderstood; for me there can be no relaxation in human company, no refined conversations, no mutual outpourings. I must live quite alone, like an outcast; I can enter society practically only as much as real necessity demands. If I approach people a burning anxiety comes over me, in that I fear being placed in danger of my condition being noticed.

It has also been like this during the last six months, which I have spent in the country. My understanding doctor, by ordering me to spare my hearing as much as possible, almost came to my own present natural disposition, although I sometimes let myself be drawn by my love of companionship. But what humiliation for me when someone standing near me heard a flute in the distance and *I heard nothing*, or someone heard the shepherd singing and again I heard nothing. Such incidents brought me almost to despair; a little more and I would have ended my life.

Only *my art* held me back. Ah, it seemed to me impossible to leave the world until I had produced all that I felt was within me; and so I spared this wretched life—truly wretched for so susceptible a body, which by a sudden change can reduce me from the best condition to the very worst.

Patience, they say, is what I must now choose for my guide, and I have done so—I hope my determination will firmly endure until it pleases the inexorable Parcae to break the thread. Perhaps I shall get better, perhaps not; I am ready.

Forced to become a philosopher already in my 28th year, it is not easy, and for the artist harder than for anyone else.

Divine One, thou lookest down on my inmost soul and knowest it; thou knowest that therein dwells the love of man and inclination to do good. O men, when at some point you read this, then consider that you have done me an injustice; and the unfortunate may console themselves to find a similar case to theirs, who despite all the limitations of nature yet did everything he could to be admitted to the ranks of worthy artists and men.

You, my brothers Carl and [Johann], as soon as I am dead, if Dr Schmidt is still alive, ask him in my name to describe my disease, and attach this written document to his account of my illness, so that at least as much as possible the world may be reconciled to me after my death.

At the same time, I here declare you two to be the heirs to my small fortune (if one can call it such); divide it fairly, and bear with and help each other. What you have done against me you know was long ago forgiven. You, brother Carl, I thank in particular for your recent proven attachment to me. My wish is that you have a better, more trouble-free life than I have had. Recommend *virtue* to your children; it alone, not money, can provide happiness. I speak from experience; virtue was what raised me in my distress. Thanks to it and to my art, I did not end my life by suicide.

> Farewell and love each other.
>
> I thank all my friends, particularly *Prince Lichnowsky* and *Professor Schmidt*—I want the instruments from Prince L. to be preserved by one of you, but not to cause strife between you; as soon as it is more useful to you, just sell them. How happy I am if I can still be of use to you in my grave—so let it be. With joy I hasten towards death. If it comes before I have had the chance to develop all my artistic abilities, then despite my harsh fate it will still be coming too soon and I should probably wish it later—yet even so I should be content, for would it not free me from a state of endless suffering? Come when thou wilt, I shall approach thee bravely.
>
> Farewell, and do not completely forget me when am dead. I have deserved this from you, since I often thought of you during my life, and of ways to make you happy; do be so.
>
> Ludwig van Beethoven
>
> Heiglnstadt [Heiligenstadt]
>
> 6 October 1802

Collaborating with Living Composers

> It is beyond important for chamber music groups to play new music and work with living composers—it is your responsibility as artists. When you have devoted the bulk of your training to studying the music of the past, the great meaning of this music is imparted when you connect it to contemporary voices. You will go back to Beethoven and Schubert with a different eye and see all the things you couldn't see before. It will make you a better performer and storyteller.
>
> ~ Gabriela Lena Frank

Look to the future and the past when choosing and studying your repertoire. There is an array of compelling contemporary chamber music and brilliant composers excited to create new works. Ensembles improve their interpretational and repertoire skills by approaching the work of living composers with the same reverence as celebrated composers from the past.

In This Section:

- Meeting the Composer
- Developing a Composer's Mindset
- Improvising: An Exercise

Meeting the Composer: Gabriela Lena Frank

> New ensembles should have active relationships with composers because a lot of the new music that is coming out now has no boundaries. And that's why the composer is there to help you.
>
> ~ Norman Fischer, cellist, Shepherd School of Music,
> Head of Chamber Music, Tanglewood Music Center,
> former member of Concord String Quartet

92 The Art of Collaboration

One of our most exciting experiences working with a living composer was at Chamber Music Accord (a summer program offered by Hartt School of Music) as a collaboration with the unforgettable composer Gabriela Lena Frank (see Figure 7.2). Young composer-instrumentalists, coached by Lena Frank, wrote a piece for their own ensemble during a 2-week-long workshop. Each composer arrived at the workshop with an unfinished piece and developed it through their interactions with the students who were to perform it.

FIGURE 7.2 Gabriela Lena Frank, composer, Director, Gabriela Lena Frank Creative Academy of Music. (Photo credit: Mariah Tauger)

It was inspiring to observe Gabriela work with these composers, encouraging them to think about how the chamber music experience enhanced their writing. They received real-time feedback from their student peer group, including the instrumentalists who performed the music and fellow student composers. Each student composer also had an immersive experience working with members of the chamber music faculty: Hyeyung Sol Yoon, Melissa Reardon, Raman Ramakrishnan, Saeunn Thorsteinsdottir, and Annie Fullard. The sparks from this experience ignited a creative transformation within each participant.

Ensembles should foray into music beyond the traditional canon—if you are lucky, you will form a lasting bond with a composer by studying and playing their work. You can use the same learning process when working on new music as more familiar music. Here is a reminder of approaches and steps to learn a new work:

- ✓ Thoroughly study the score in addition to learning your part.
- ✓ Be attentive to all musical details and make notes about words or indications which need research.

✓ Research new techniques and musical language by listening to recordings of the work, contacting the composer, or contacting performers who worked on the piece.

Develop relationships with living composers and explore composers in your community and region (Box 7.3). Here are some for consideration: Gabriela Lena Frank, Osvaldo Golijov, Eric Gould, Jessie Montgomery, Daniel Bernard Romain, Caroline Shaw, Jerod Impichchaachaaha' Tate, Joan Tower, Michi Wiancko, Paul Wiancko, and Dinuk Wijeratne. Explore Appendix A for reference sources for underrepresented composers.

Box 7.3 Advice from Gabriela Lena Frank on Working with Living Composers

✓ Most of the time, composers of the past wrote pieces of music for a specific group, for performers whose quirks they really knew. So, when you work with a living composer, suddenly you have that perspective. It recalibrates your brain and refreshes you.

✓ The first time a quartet gets together to read through something, composers should not be there. I don't think they should even be there the second time. During the first meeting, depending on what the timeline is for the performance, the performers can start to find and highlight their favorite moments in the piece. When you highlight your favorite moments, then your individual interpretation starts to come together, and you have something to offer to the composer. This process is more useful for the players and results in an elevated conversation.

✓ Try to have two shorter rehearsals with the composer rather than one long rehearsal. It gives time for the performers to put into place some of the suggestions of the composer.

✓ For composers, be mindful of the skill sets of the performers, and respectful of what they want to communicate. If there are aspects of the music that are uncomfortable, you can bring them up, but there is a way to do so with humor and compassion. The performers should try the suggestions of the composer, and the composer should acknowledge the players' willingness to experiment with the composer's ideas.

Developing a Composer's Mindset

It's a different way of thinking when you are working with composers on a regular basis. Ensembles in the second half of the twentieth century that had active relationships with composers, such as the Juilliard Quartet, had to be broadly stylistically conscious.

~ Norman Fischer, cellist, Shepherd School of Music,
Head of Chamber Music, Tanglewood Music Center,
former member of Concord String Quartet

94 The Art of Collaboration

Develop a composer's mindset to visualize what you want to express beyond the composer's instructions before you play a piece. Performers design a musical journey for their audience based on an overall vision. By thinking like a composer, performers relate to their music as if they are creating it, humanizing the interpretation experience. Imagine that you wrote the work yourself and envision what your inspiration and intent may have been.

Developing a Composer's Mindset Through Improvisation

When working off the printed page, there should be a sense of improvisation to allow for the spontaneous expression of the musical imagination. Once you have done your research, study, and preparation, pay attention to your intuitive senses to inform your interpretation.

First, be curious and listen to different examples of free improvisation to open your senses, such as Indian Classical music and music from East Asia, Afghanistan, and Syria. Listen to artists such as Charlie Parker, Miles Davis, Bill Evans, John Coltrane, and Thelonious Monk, who created the blueprint for jazz improvisation. European composers such as J. S. Bach, W. A. Mozart, Felix Mendelssohn, and Ludwig van Beethoven have been recognized for their extraordinary improvisational skills. You can listen to performers today who create their own cadenzas for the concerti of these composers.

When approaching music intuitively, the character, tonality, and rhythm are sources of inspiration. Listening with openness and spontaneity leads to a rich, interwoven group performing experience. The exercise in the next section helps develop trust in your musical and intuitive senses, inspired by Constance Barrett[6] and used extensively by Deborah Barrett Price, founder and Director of Chamber Music Connection, Columbus, Ohio. The Cavani Quartet and Deborah Price have collaborated for many years. Deborah's sister, Constance Barrett, cellist, innovated this improvisation exercise as an icebreaker and chamber music warmup. It can be adapted in many ways, and a modified version is detailed in the following section.

Improvising Together: An Exercise

> Improvisation is a part of the experience and often involves a lot less talking. A sign of a good rehearsal is when you don't have to say anything, because things are clicking and you're communicating nonverbally. In an improvisational mindset, rehearsal is about exploring a lot of options, any of which might...happen on stage.
>
> ~ Mike Block, cellist, Silk Road Ensemble

The intention of this exercise is to explore free expression through listening and co-creating a synchronized experience. The entire experience should be practiced

Exploring the Composer's World   95

nonverbally. Improvising together requires that you watch each other closely for each entrance. Players are encouraged to let go of judgment, adopt a composer's mindset, and have fun!

This exercise is designed to work with a small ensemble. If you are working with a larger group, you can subdivide it into smaller groups of 3–5 members. Our example is for four players—however, you can adapt this exercise for any number of players in a small group.

1. Form a circle, facing each other, without music stands.
2. Create a moment of silence before beginning.
3. Amid the silence, whoever feels inspired (any instrument) can begin. Play a repeated rhythm of your choice (*ostinato*)—any dynamic, tempo, or combination of notes.
4. After the *ostinato* is repeated several times, the next member joins in with their choice of sound effect, synchronizing rhythm with the *ostinato*. Sound effects can take the form of a slide between two notes (*glissando*), a percussive sound on their instrument, tapping fingers on the instrument, or for string players, different bow techniques, for example, *col legno* or *ponticello*—or for wind players, you can make sounds with only the mouthpiece.
5. The next member adds a melodic group of notes, synchronizing rhythm with the *ostinato*. This melody can be any notes in any range of the instrument and can be as simple as the first three notes of a scale, ascending and descending.
6. The fourth member also chooses their melodic material, adding a mood or emotional quality. To express the melody in a joyful and triumphant mood, you might play *forte* with enthusiasm and a smile. Alternatively, you could play a soft, minor melody to evoke melancholy. You are your inner expressive actor by exaggerating your physical motions to enable everyone in the group to understand and imitate the mood.
7. Everyone in the group matches the mood of the final player. Continue with your group improvisation for a few seconds, then pause (laughter is encouraged).
8. Begin again, with a new person initiating the *ostinato*, and repeat the process. This exercise could also be done without instruments, using vocal and body percussion.

This chapter presented an approach to find interpretive inspiration by gaining deeper insight into the context of composers' lives. Parts I, II, and III lay the foundation for the rehearsal techniques found in Part IV. This foundation guides decisions regarding when and why to employ the rehearsal techniques and strategies in Part IV.

PART IV
TECHNIQUES FOR PRODUCTIVE REHEARSALS

I am lucky to have had incredible mentors in my life, and the Cavani Quartet is the most important. I still rely on many of the wonderful techniques I learned from them, including left hand coordination, breathing and movement exercises, and Shakespearean counting. My quartet has adopted these as great teaching tools and share them when we teach and collaborate. The Cavani Quartet is the reason I have a career in chamber music today.

~ Karla Donehew Perez, member, Catalyst Quartet

In Part IV:

Chapter 8: Techniques for Cueing and Breathing Together
Chapter 9: Techniques for Rhythmic Alignment and Ensemble
Chapter 10: Techniques for Intonation
Chapter 11: Techniques for Sound Production
Chapter 12: Techniques for Projecting Expression
Chapter 13: Techniques for Strategic Listening and Balance
Chapter 14: The Capstone Technique: *Live, Breathe, and Die* (*LBAD*)

Part IV presents essential and practical techniques, organized by their intended purpose, for everyday use in rehearsals and teaching. These techniques are designed to give each ensemble member an equal voice in the interpretive process and help solve technical issues. This part provides a wealth of options to address the challenges of ensemble playing—if a particular technique does not work for your group, try another.

The strategies and techniques in these final chapters help to alleviate conflict and shift the culture of group interactions to a positive, collaborative, and goal-oriented rehearsal process. The final chapter offers a transformative technique called *LBAD* (Live, Breathe, and Die), empowering nonverbal communication between ensemble members and generating a reciprocal thread of musical conversation.

8

TECHNIQUES FOR CUEING AND BREATHING TOGETHER

> You are an organic part of the body, the heartbeat from deep down inside
> part of the work . . . you are setting the pulse
> ~ Peter Salaff, former member, Cleveland String Quartet

In This Chapter:

- Sharing the Cueing Responsibility
- Pantomime Cueing
- Conducting and Breathing Together
- Cueing with Instruments

Cueing and breathing together are fundamental skills for playing chamber music and are a shared responsibility of ensemble members. It is helpful for each ensemble member to understand and assume the responsibilities associated with being a great conductor, which include rhythmic clarity and character projection. A skilled conductor uses the power of their physical motion, which serves as a *cue* to inspire the collective expression of the music. Great cues initiate with a breath.

Cueing establishes rhythmic precision and expands group awareness. Cueing develops the ability to communicate through physical motion. A cue should indicate the character, the dynamic, and the rhythmic pulse. Cueing and breathing together enhances the "initiate and respond" nature of chamber music playing. Former Cavani Quartet member Merry Peckham uses the descriptive term *Über Cue* to emphasize the enthusiasm, energy, and physical movement which clearly illustrate the tempo and character of the music.

There are a variety of effective techniques that can be used during rehearsals to improve the group's rhythm and to allow each member to physically embody the character of the music. When a group utilizes such techniques, a process called *entrainment* occurs.

The phenomenon of entrainment was discovered by the Dutch scientist Christiaan Huygens in the seventeenth century when he noticed that the rhythms of pendulum clocks placed in the same room naturally align with a common rhythmic cycle.[1] Similarly, when synchronized musicians perform music together, their breath and other physiological systems align, or entrain, as shown by recent scientific studies. The group that moves together, plays together!

The Art of Collaboration. Annie Fullard and Dorianne Cotter-Lockard, Oxford University Press. © Oxford University Press 2025.
DOI: 10.1093/oso/9780197673126.003.0009

During the past 15–20 years, several noted music scholars have researched and written about the importance of understanding the relationship between music and gesture.[2] From this research and personal experience, we have developed the following techniques that improve the rhythmic precision of an ensemble through the use of expressive movement. Following the progression of techniques below will not only enhance the performance of your ensemble but will also further develop your cueing skills.

Sharing the Cueing Responsibility: Initiator and Inspirer

> It is like a family speaking with each other. If a passage goes from the first, second, or cello, there is a contact, sometimes it is visual. It can be a sense of opening and feeling a tremendous closeness to the person with whom you have the solo. Like in a family sitting at a dining room table, you move, discussing something with one person, and then discussing with another. The whole time you're aware of the other person and their feelings.
> ~ Martha Strongin Katz, former member, Cleveland String Quartet

The person giving the cue is the *main initiator* or *main inspirer*. These terms help avoid the implication that one person is leading while the others are following. Ideally, all players should participate in rhythmic initiation, where *everyone* gives and reflects cues at the same time.

Interestingly, the word *initiate* implies movement, while the word *inspire* is derived from the Latin word *inspirare*, which means to breathe. In each of our rehearsals and performances, ensemble members aim to inspire each other to move and breathe as one unit. Below are some guidelines for using these techniques:

✓ The musical decision regarding who becomes the main initiator is typically based on which instrument has the melody or main motif. In other words, the person with the principal material generally initiates the cue.

✓ If no instrument has the melody, the main initiator can be the person with the downbeat, or the person with the rhythmic subdivisions.

✓ Take turns experimenting with different members initiating (see *LBAD* technique).

✓ We recommend the practice of cueing and breathing yourself in after every rest—this generates rhythmic energy and musical vitality, helping the group to stay together.

✓ Regardless of the role you are playing, it is tremendously important that *each member of the ensemble* breathes and cues themselves in after a rest.

Pantomime Cueing: Finding Your "Inner Conductor"

> You are setting a pulse . . . that creates a river in which a melody can glide. The inner voices are very important in creating a feeling of excitement and fire. I often think of it like a human body, where one person is the lungs and another is the heart, and everyone has to take part in the blood flow and the circulation, so it comes to life. It is alive!
>
> ~ Peter Salaff, former member, Cleveland String Quartet

The goal of this technique is to establish a unified entrance by cueing without instruments. This involves a pantomime of the physical gesture of a conductor's cue (see Figure 8.1).

The following steps outline how to cue one downbeat entrance together:

1. Set your instruments down in a safe place.
2. Sit on the edge of your chairs or stand in an engaged stance.
3. Each ensemble member takes a turn serving as "the main conductor," while other members mirror their gestures and breathing.
4. Drawing on the *ready position* in sports, imagine that you are a basketball player about to pass the ball, or a tennis player about to return a serve. In the same way, ensemble members should get into a ready position, considering the posture of the body and the position of the instrument, allowing the musicians to be fully engaged in the musical moment.

FIGURE 8.1 Rafael Payere giving a cue. (Photo Credit: Antoine Saito)

102   The Art of Collaboration

5. Imagine that everyone in the ensemble has a baton in their hand. Hold your own hands as if ready to conduct.
6. Imagine the tempo you all wish to play.
7. The main initiator should ensure that everyone makes eye contact before the group initiates the cue.
8. Everyone breathes in with the initiator and pantomimes the cue simultaneously by moving their hands upward so that the tempo is clear in the preparatory gesture (which is referred to as *the upbeat*).
9. Everyone mirrors the main initiator's cue and conducting motions as they breathe out together (this is referred to as *the downbeat*).
10. Once you have synchronized cueing and breathing together without instruments, you can practice these steps with your instruments.

This technique develops each members' confidence in their cueing abilities. It greatly improves rhythmic accuracy and solidifies the musical commitment of the ensemble. While the exercise is especially helpful at the beginnings and endings of works, it is a vital tool for showing entrances after a rest, or at dramatic musical points such as moments of extreme dynamic contrast, after a *fermata* (𝄐), or *grand pause*. The next step is to extend beyond cueing a single note by conducting and breathing together without instruments, through entire phrases.

Conducting and Breathing Together

The cue defines tempo, dynamics, and character. Use the following technique to understand and agree on tempos, develop the rhythmic character and interpretation of a section, and align together rhythmically. There are many online videos available to observe conductors. Watch how they use their hands, body, and face to express the music and communicate with their colleagues. Communicating with physical expression is integral to playing chamber music. Therefore, exaggerate your body movements and facial expressions when practicing cueing (see video of Leonard Bernstein conducting only with his face).[3]

Figure 8.2 shows some basic beat patterns every instrumentalist should know to express rhythmic character through their hands.

Practice the following steps without instruments:

1. Choose a passage of music to use for this activity.
2. Determine the appropriate beat pattern for the passage. Focus on the musical gesture rather than replicating the pattern precisely.
3. Each person takes a turn initiating as conductor. Be dramatic; conduct your interpretation of the character of the music.
4. All group members mirror the initiator through the passage, conducting along with the initiator.

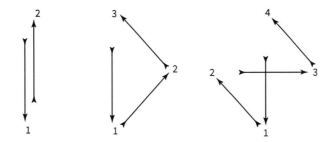

FIGURE 8.2 Diagrams of 2, 3, and 4 beat patterns. Source: https://en.wikipedia.org/wiki/Conducting

5. After all ensemble members have had a turn to conduct, discuss the different interpretations of the *tempo*, articulation, and character.
6. *Variations*: Conduct while playing, singing, or while listening to a recording.

Cueing with Your Instruments

> I often will look at our horn player, I'll focus on his embouchure, and I can see how it is about to set and how he breathes in, so I follow that.
> ~ Monica Ellis, bassoon, Imani Winds

Eric Wong, former violist of the Cavani Quartet, refers to the cue as "breathing yourself in." In other words, you are to connect your breath with your entire body. While this is natural for wind and brass players and singers, it may take some extra practice for others. For string players, it can be helpful to think of connecting your breathing to your bow arm, feeling the natural weight of your right hand as you connect your bow with the string.

In This Section:
- Zone of Silence
- Cueing for Wind and Brass Players
- Helpful Hints

Using the Zone of Silence

It is essential to use silence to create the right atmosphere before you breathe and cue. You will want to use silence at both the beginning and end of movements to captivate your audience with the drama of the music. Think of movement beginnings and endings as a picture frame around a beautiful work of art. Our former cellist, Merry Peckham, calls this the *zone of silence*.

1. Before the cue create the *zone of silence*, using your physical posture. This moment of stillness is as important as the cue itself—imagine the rhythm and tempo during the silence before you give the cue.

104   The Art of Collaboration

2. Breathe together before you begin. Try what we refer to as *the chamber music sniff* to cue. Avoid snorting!

3. While breathing together, cue through physical motion. The movement originates from the back. As you move, be aware of the power and strength of your entire body.

4. With your instruments, duplicate the musical gesture that you made during the conducting pantomime.

5. Begin by practicing cueing and breathing only the downbeat together with instruments while each person takes a turn initiating the cue.

6. Finally, cue simultaneously and continue to play the passage.

Cueing for Wind and Brass Players

Monica Ellis, founder of Imani Winds and Jeff Scott, former member, Imani Winds, teach their students to move their instruments in a beat pattern as if they are conducting. Although it is easier for a flute, clarinet, or oboe to conduct beat patterns with their instrument than for a bassoon or French horn player, conducting beat patterns with instruments is an effective technique for wind and brass ensembles.

For cueing entrances, brass instruments make their sound in a similar manner, using a mouthpiece. When air moves through a horn, the note begins. For reed players, everything happens inside the mouth, making it difficult to know when the note is about to sound. Therefore, Ellis and Scott recommend that in a wind quintet, it is essential to learn how each instrument produces sound.

The first step is to learn about the embouchure for each instrument, such as how much wind is used to make sound and how articulations are made. In addition, it is important to recognize the connection of the breath along with the engagement of the diaphragm, abdomen, and lower back muscles. All these elements go into the unique production of sound for each instrument. Make it a practice to observe how each person creates sound. This awareness not only gives you a deeper appreciation for your fellow musicians, but also helps in understanding what you need to do with your instrument to successfully play together.

Because of the unique pedagogy for different instruments, musicians learn how to breathe in a variety of ways. An efficient breathing technique for one instrument may be less efficient for another. For woodwind and brass players, it is important to develop an awareness of how breathing for each instrument affects the cue.

Helpful Hints on Cueing

Below are some additional helpful hints for implementing your cueing skills in both individual and ensemble practice.

Individual Practice

We recommend incorporating cueing techniques in warmups, scales, arpeggios, and your solo repertoire. Choose your tempo, articulation, dynamic, and character before you begin playing, and indicate these ideas in your cue. Make sure to be expressive and creative! Adding this exercise to your scale and arpeggio practice results in a mindful and productive process.

When practicing solo repertoire such as sonatas, showpieces, or concertos, it is essential to think of these works as chamber music—become aware of how your part fits with the piano or the orchestra.

Furthermore, practice embodying the rhythmic character of your entrances. Imagine the other part or parts playing before you enter—be aware of the dynamics, articulation, tempo, mood, and style or genre of music. Imagine the sound you wish to make, and let your cue embody that sound.

In unaccompanied repertoire, such as solo Bach, think of playing chamber music with yourself by using voicing. If you are a string player, approach each string as a different timbre or voice and create a counterpoint and dialogue between them. Cueing yourself at phrase beginnings and endings illuminates a clear musical structure and changes of character.

As you play, pretend you are reading a poem to your audience, thinking about nuance, inflection, pauses, and the energy of sound moving through the room. Remember that there is always enough time to breathe and cue in any musical phrase.

Ensemble Practice

In ensemble playing, there are numerous examples of musical moments when the ensemble must unite their focus and cue together. Cueing includes visual connection between ensemble members. We describe these moments as *being up*, meaning each person holds a ready and attentive posture while looking at other members of the group.

The following are moments where everyone must cue together, using the center of the group as a focal point:

- ✓ Beginnings of phrases
- ✓ Cadence points and phrase endings
- ✓ Climactic moments
- ✓ Changes in harmony or key
- ✓ *Subito* (sudden) dynamic changes
- ✓ Transitions: *ritardando* (slowing down) and *accelerando* (speeding up)
- ✓ After a rest, *fermata*, or *grand pause*
- ✓ For slow music, cue on the implied rhythmic beats. The implied rhythm is the beat before any note changes.
- ✓ For fast music, cueing together at strategic points helps to unify the pulse and synchronize fast passages.

106 The Art of Collaboration

✓ For abrupt character changes, freeze your bodies in the character of the last note you played. Allow for time to cue in the new character. This will ensure that you play together and will clearly delineate character changes for your audience.

Final Hints

Be patient, and experiment with a variety of physical movements until you become comfortable showing rhythmic character. With practice, your cueing skills will become a natural and organic part of your playing and offer a means to expand your expressive and musical capabilities.

✓ Watch and learn from great conductors.
✓ Watch and learn from artists you admire.
✓ Watch and learn from your colleagues!

9

TECHNIQUES FOR RHYTHMIC ALIGNMENT AND ENSEMBLE

> In order to share the music, you play with each other and the audience, one must have awareness of what to do technically, physically, and logistically.
> ~ Joel Krosnick, former member, Juilliard String Quartet

In This Chapter:

- Synchronizing Movement—*Chamber Music Aerobics*
- Expressive Counting—*Shakespearean Counting*
- Using the Metronome
- Visual Connection
- Passing the Melody or Motive
- Exaggerating Tempos
- Clapping (Composite Rhythms and Syncopation)
- *Left Hands Alone* (Tactile Synchronization)
- Creating *Rubato* Through Agogic Playing

This chapter contains techniques to improve group rhythm and ensemble alignment. Many involve using physical motion to convey rhythmic character. Physically embodying the character of the music as you play leads to cohesion and more expressive music-making.

During the past 15–20 years, music scholars have researched and written about the importance of understanding music and gesture.[1] The following techniques use body movement and physical gestures as an interpretive tool. Cavani Quartet members have implemented these techniques over many years of successful chamber music coaching to demonstrate greater rhythmic precision through expressive movement.

In addition to the techniques in this chapter, the BAPNE Method (Biomecánica. Anatomía. Psicología. Neurociencia. Etnomusicología: Biomechanics, Anatomy, Psychology, Neuroscience, Ethnomusicology) and Dalcroze eurhythmics provide a deeper exploration of expressing rhythm through the body.[2]

The Art of Collaboration. Annie Fullard and Dorianne Cotter-Lockard, Oxford University Press. © Oxford University Press 2025.
DOI: 10.1093/oso/9780197673126.003.0010

Synchronizing Your Movement: *Chamber Music Aerobics*

Chamber Music Aerobics is a favorite technique for synchronizing rhythm and solving issues without argument in small and larger ensembles. It can also be adapted as a coaching strategy to empower students to be physically expressive.

Chamber Music Aerobics is symbolic of the physical nature of this rehearsal technique, as the experience is kinesthetic and sensory, freeing the body and creating a whole-body resonance. As a result, the ensemble sound expands, and the group develops improved connection and awareness.

This technique positively affects group dynamics by encouraging ensemble members to communicate nonverbally, synchronize, respond, and become more aware of each other. Laughter is often involved, helping diffuse tension when a group struggles to play together. Since ensemble members gain confidence when they learn to show rhythm and character, moving expressively and embodying rhythmic character are vital to chamber music playing.

The objective is to *move together* with a regular pulse and become a human metronome. Imagine you are the pendulum of the metronome. As you practice this technique, imagine gathering energy from the ground up through your body. Here are some helpful hints:

- ✓ Choose a tempo as indicated by the composer's marking or the appropriate tempo for the character (e.g., *allegro moderato*).
- ✓ Move together on every downbeat and in the middle of the bar if it is a slow tempo.
- ✓ Watch each other to make sure you are moving simultaneously—as if connected by a virtual rubber band.
- ✓ The movement should reflect the character of the passage.

This technique may feel awkward at first, but the simplicity of moving simultaneously is fundamental to creating an embodied group rhythm. Here are the steps to practice this technique:

1. First, move together in a synchronized pulse from RIGHT to LEFT, while holding your instrument in playing position but without playing.
2. Then, move together from RIGHT to LEFT while playing the passage with your instruments.
3. Next, move your upper body forward (DOWN) and backward (UP) to the pulse while holding your instrument in playing position but without playing. Cellists will initiate this movement from the neck to the top of the head. This is called "the noble nod."
5. Then, move together DOWN and UP while playing the passage with instruments.
6. Next, move in a CLOCKWISE or CIRCULAR MOTION without playing. Move forward, go to the right, go to the back, and then to the left.

7. Then, try this circular motion while playing the passage.
8. Finally, experiment with natural movements which show the pulse, express the musical intent, and help the group to synchronize.

Expressive Counting: *Shakespearean Counting*

As a young player, you practice alone. You take lessons alone. You may never have been in a musical conversation. When you get into a chamber music group for the first time, it may be a unique experience to play your part in response to someone else. It may seem like your colleague is saying the "same words" in a different way. You're not giving a speech. You are taking part in a conversation.

~ Joel Krosnick, former member, Juilliard String Quartet

Expressive Counting, also referred to as *Shakespearean Counting* enables ensemble members to engage in the conversation by using the voice and body in a theatrical way, without the technical constraints of instruments. It is an effective technique for unifying rhythm—the Cavani Quartet uses it all the time!

This technique aligns the group rhythmically, helping ensemble members to understand the dynamics, articulation, and character of a piece (see Figure 9.1). This technique has an equalizing effect on group relationships as everyone breathes and speaks the music together. It unifies the group and is FUN!

FIGURE 9.1 Annie Fullard, demonstrating Shakespearean Counting. (Photo Credit: Andie Wolf)

Here are the steps to practice *Expressive (Shakespearean) Counting*:

1. Choose a passage to work on without your instruments.

110　The Art of Collaboration

2. Count the numbers (beats) in each measure *out loud, all together*. For example, you may say: "one and, two and, three and, four and . . ."
3. Count with dynamics.
4. Become a Shakespearean actor!
   - Speak with articulation, confidence, and intention.
   - Enunciate your "words."
   - Project your character to your colleagues—exaggerate gestures.
5. Ensure the style and vocal inflection represent the composer's musical intentions.

You may be self-conscious the first time you try this technique. However, once you are comfortable with a theatrical, expressive counting approach, this technique results in major improvements for ensemble playing. Here are a few variations to try:

✓ Stand up and count your parts while physically embodying the character, as if having a conversation.
✓ Use gestures that imply reaching across and connecting with your colleagues.
✓ By standing as if you are an actor on the stage, you can illuminate the musical ideas with greater expression.

The Metronome Is Your Friend

> Anyone who knows how much is at stake in observing the proper tempo called for by any piece of music, and what great errors can arise in the process, will not doubt this imperative. If one has specific rules for this, and if one were to obey them dutifully, then . . . a piece which is often distorted by an improper tempo would have a much better effect, and would accord its composer more honor than is often the case.
>
> ~ Johann Joachim Quantz, 1752

Use the metronome as a resource to establish tempos related to the character of the music. From Beethoven's era onward, composers often indicated metronome markings in the score. However, if there are no metronome markings, begin by researching the style and context of the work. Then, you can listen to several recordings by different artists to reference examples of tempo interpretation. A wealth of information is available on composers and their tempo choices (see articles by Levin and Kolisch on Beethoven's tempos in *Musical Quarterly*).[3,4]

Using the metronome during rehearsal aligns rhythms and ensures precision and consistency across the ensemble. For string players, the metronome helps to develop a strong, even left hand. Listening to the metronome pulse helps string players to organize their bow speed and pressure. For brass, woodwinds, and vocalists, it can help with breathing and phrasing. It is best to use the metronome individually before coming to the rehearsal. While the metronome is a practical device, it is one of many ways to attain rhythmic synchrony. Remember that the end goal is to convey the character of the music. Here are the steps to incorporate the metronome:

1. Start by observing the markings at the top of a movement. For example, *Allegro*, *Presto*, *Largo*, or *Adagio* indicate the composer's intent for the mood and tempo.
2. Play the passage with the metronome set to major beats or subdivisions in the desired tempo.
3. Rather than always playing along with the metronome, listen to the tempo from the metronome and move your body with the pulse for a few moments before beginning to play.
4. Turn the metronome off and try to feel the pulse together without the aid of the metronome.
5. IMPORTANT: Once you have established a consistent pulse, look for all places in the music where it should breathe. You will want to allocate more time to expressive gestures such as dynamic changes, climaxes, harmonic changes, and cadences (see the *Live, Breathe, and Die* technique).

Establishing Visual Connection: Look Up Once per Measure

At its core, chamber music is the process of engaging in brilliant musical conversations. In addition to active listening, maintaining a visual relationship with other ensemble members helps with the technical aspects of playing together. When audience members witness performers who visually connect with each other, they find the experience transformative and compelling.

Liberating ourselves from the music on the stand frees us to engage with each other in real time, and visual connection becomes a natural part of the performance. In live theater, actors maintain visual connection with their colleagues to demonstrate the relationships between characters in a play. In team sports, players must maintain a visual connection to each other to score points, pass the ball, or assist a goal.

The goal is to give your attention to your colleagues as much as possible and express the composer's intentions. Visual connection takes practice and becomes a habit when you are comfortable with your part and how it fits with the others.

Using a low, lightweight stand, follow these steps to practice visual connection:

1. A good way to develop your visual connection skill is to look up once per bar.
2. Place your visual attention on who is playing the melody or main motif.

3. Find your "rhythm buddy" by focusing on who is playing the same rhythm to ensure you are synchronized (see the *Score Study* chapter).
4. Play a passage or a section by memory (by heart).

Playing by memory is liberating and allows the music to soar! This is not to say that performing by memory is a requirement—it is simply a way to deepen the ensemble connection.

Passing the Melody or Motive

> I have a similar coaching style to the Cavanis in that I'm very intense about passing lines, sensing each other, communicating between each other, and predicting in advance where the next person is going to put the next note, which I think is one of the most exhilarating aspects of playing chamber music.
>
> ~ Vivian Hornik Weilerstein: pianist, Director Professional
> Piano Trio Program, piano and collaborative piano faculty,
> New England Conservatory of Music

One of the more joyful aspects of playing chamber music is exchanging ideas through nonverbal communication. This technique combines physical and aural skills. Beloved composers, such as Haydn, Beethoven, and Bartók, and creative contemporary living composers, such as Joan Tower and Jessie Montgomery, delight in exploring the timbres and ranges of each instrument by passing the melody or motives around the ensemble and highlighting each.

Demonstrating this technique physically and visually helps the rehearsal process and creates performances that fully engage your listener in musical dialogue. First, clearly identify the melody or motive as it passes around the ensemble, using the score to understand how each part interacts and synchronizes. One approach is to play from the score, but an even more powerful approach is to write cues into individual parts, identifying the names of players or instruments with the melody or main motive (see the chapter "Score Study").

The best way to illustrate this technique is through a sports metaphor. Visualize how basketball players work together when they assist a team member in making a shot. As the ball passes from one player to another, there is heightened awareness and active physical motion between them. At the highest level of ensemble playing, this technique becomes a rhythmic dance, with each player responding to the other to achieve a cohesive musical gesture. For a group of musicians without a conductor, passing the melody or motive with active movement around the ensemble is a transformative experience.

From a pedagogical standpoint, this technique is often the Cavani Quartet's first approach when working with young ensembles. Passing the melody helps groups to discover the conversational aspects of the music and value the importance of non-verbal communication.

Imagine raising your hand and pointing to the voice which has the melody—you can even do this as an exercise in the rehearsal. Actively focus on the melodic voice through visual contact with the player. In rehearsal and performance, this technique increases attention to ensemble dynamics, rhythmic alignment, and articulation. It takes a bit of practice, but the result is a more energetic and spontaneous performance.

The following four excerpts of passages from three well-known composers illustrate different examples of passing the melody. In Figure 9.2, Joseph Haydn's String Quartet Opus 76, No 5, *Presto*, is an example of how Haydn thrills the listener with quicksilver passagework which passes around the quartet and offers each instrument a chance to play a version of the motive. In the opening, Haydn tosses the motive in the opening between the violin in a high register and the cello in a low register.

FIGURE 9.2 Motive passed between violin 1 and cello. Haydn String Quartet in D Major, Op.76, No. 5, Presto.

In Figure 9.3, at measure 255 of Haydn's String Quartet Opus 76, the motive is passed from the viola to the second violin and then to the first violin.

FIGURE 9.3 Haydn Opus 76, No 5, Presto. Transformed motive passed between viola, violin 2, and violin 1.

In the opening of the first movement of Dvořák's String Quartet, Opus 96, the melody begins with the viola, passes to violin 1, and then passes through the entire quartet in a wonderful cascade of sixteenth notes (see Figure 9.4).

FIGURE 9.4 Pass the melody. Dvořák String Quartet in F Major, Op.96, "American," Allegro ma non troppo.

Since this passage can be difficult to execute, the best approach is to perform it in slow motion, playing only the sixteenth notes. Exaggerate the physical motion of passing the melody by leaning toward the player who plays the sixteenth notes after you. The order as shown in the score is cello to violin 2, then to violin 1, and finally to viola. Once you have played through slowly while exaggerating the connection between the players, perform the passage up to tempo, and enjoy the newfound energy. This passage immediately repeats itself in a minor key—be sure to feel the change of mood and sonorities as you pass the sixteenth notes around (see measures 11–14 above).

Beethoven's Opus 135 is an extraordinary work—it is the last quartet Beethoven wrote, and perhaps the most complicated to interpret, yet the most compact in length. Beethoven uses an agglomeration of motives which float from voice to voice so quickly that it can be difficult to follow. The opening movement is an animated conversation—a highly organized stream of consciousness. In performance, the interplay of motives is wonderful to listen to and behold.

By approaching the first movement of Opus 135 by passing the melody throughout, it deepens understanding of the musical rhetoric and the way the music speaks. In addition, this technique can help with rhythmic alignment (see Figure 9.5 for an example of the opening).

FIGURE 9.5 Beethoven String Quartet in F Major, Op.135, Allegretto.

The more you use this technique to recognize the connection between the parts, the more natural it will be to lean toward each ensemble member as you pass the melody. This technique creates a seamless and vibrant interpretation, resulting in a more spontaneous and electrifying performance.

Synchronizing Rhythmic Subdivisions

Rhythmic alignment occurs when players understand how the note values in their part relate to the smaller subdivisions within the score. The technique requires that one or more ensemble members play rhythmic subdivisions of their notes while others play the passage as written. This section includes two examples:

- ✓ One individual has a fast passage, and the other members play longer note values.
- ✓ Playing a passage marked with a slow tempo when the score does not contain rhythmic subdivisions.

Although these examples are from the string quartet literature, ensembles can implement this technique for any combination of instruments and musical style. In Figure 9.6, in the first movement of Haydn Op. 76 No. 2 in d minor ("Quinten"), measures 63–73, the second violinist, violist, and cellist play sixteenth notes where half notes are written. This means playing simultaneously with the first violinist, who has sixteenth notes in their part, lining up the subdivisions.

FIGURE 9.6 Haydn String Quartet in d minor, Op. 76 No. 2, "Quinten," Allegro.

In Figure 9.7, Mendelssohn Quartet, Opus 13 in a minor, Adagio, measures 1–13, subdivide the passage with eighth notes using the bowing and rhythms as marked in the score. For example, in the first phrase, subdivide rhythms by playing eighth notes. Doing so improves bow distribution and contact point while unifying rhythm and sound.

FIGURE 9.7 Mendelssohn String Quartet in a minor, Op. 13, Adagio, measures 1–13.

Here are some helpful hints regarding this technique:

✓ Use the metronome as a tool to help the ensemble to maintain a consistent tempo.

Techniques for Rhythmic Alignment and Ensemble   **117**

✓ Take turns during which one person plays the small subdivisions while the rest of the ensemble members perform the passage as written.

✓ Agree on a common interpretation of the subdivisions the group feels when performing a particular passage. For example, group members can feel a 4/4 measure in quarter notes, eighth notes, or even half notes.

Exaggerating Tempos

Exaggerating the tempo develops greater awareness of harmonies, rhythms, and phrasing. This technique includes playing in slow motion, playing at hyper-speed, and achieving a long line. To implement these techniques, it is critical to understand the function of meter in music.

> **In This Section:**
>
> - Playing in Slow Motion
> - Playing at Hyper-Speed
> - Achieving a Long Line

According to *Oxford University Dictionary of Music*, meter is "the organization of a regular succession of rhythmical impulses, or beats, for example, 3/4 and 6/8 being described as different kinds."[5] Meter is distinct from rhythm in that it provides the underlying framework of pulses and accents against which a particular rhythm is defined.

Many systems of musical meter exist around the world. For example, African, Arabic, and Indian music have their own systems for organizing rhythm. Western music developed the concept of meter from poetry. An early system of rhythmic notation in Western music was derived from rhythmic modes in the meter of classical ancient Greek and Latin poetry.[6]

Playing in Slow Motion: *Discovery Tempo*

Playing in slow motion is extremely helpful for lining up rhythms. We refer to this as a *discovery tempo*, a term borrowed from the Verona String Quartet. Play through a fast movement in slow motion to focus your listening. This technique is analogous to looking at something under a microscope, as it helps to discern complex rhythms. To practice, begin with two players at a time.

This technique works well in progressive steps. Start with a very slow tempo, then a medium tempo, and finally try a tempo that is about two-thirds of the indicated tempo.

Playing at Hyper-Speed

Playing in *hyper-speed* can develop a longer phrase line and enables the flow of the music. Play the passage much faster than the marked tempo—even double the

118 The Art of Collaboration

speed—to hear the arc of the phrase and produce a longer musical line. This technique is especially helpful in slower passages where the *tempo* feels like it is dragging.

Achieving a Long Line

Inspired by the ideas of cellist and humanitarian Pablo Casals, Peter Salaff described the process of achieving a *long line* as a magnet pulling you as an ensemble toward a "special point" in the music.[7] The following exercise will help you discover the harmonic and rhythmic movement that illuminates the long line, expanding your perspective and awareness of a larger musical framework.

Play only the downbeats of a passage in progression. Think of using hypermeter—meaning to feel the downbeats of each whole measure—rather than the individual rhythms in each measure. Ensembles that move together on a larger pulse (hypermeter) unify musical direction and rhythmic alignment. It is as if you are climbing a mountain together from plateau to plateau, moving as an entrained unit. Next, play the passage as written, aiming toward the special points in the music.

Clapping Rhythms Together

> **In This Section:**
> - Composite Rhythms
> - Syncopation

Clapping establishes rhythmic pulse, alignment, and connection between ensemble members without the use of instruments, focusing only on the rhythms. Clap the rhythm for all four parts as if the group were playing the passage with instruments. You can also tap your leg if you prefer not to clap.

Playing Composite Rhythms

A composite rhythm is a pattern formed by merging separate rhythms in each part into an integrated whole. White defines composite rhythm as "the resultant overall rhythmic articulation among all the voices of a contrapuntal texture."[8] This technique requires playing from the score. By following these steps, ensembles can illuminate complex rhythmic passages clearly and cohesively, and rehearsals will be more productive.

1. Practice the passage without instruments, with each ensemble member clapping their part under tempo.
2. Clap everyone's part from the score to produce a composite rhythm.
3. While clapping, exaggerate passing the rhythm around the group.

Techniques for Rhythmic Alignment and Ensemble   119

4. With instruments, play the passage under tempo, followed by the tempo indicated.

In Figure 9.8, Haydn's Quartet Op. 76, no 4, "Sunrise," IV. *Finale*, measures 110–121 illustrate a passage containing a composite rhythm where a melodic line is passed from one instrument to the next without interruption.

FIGURE 9.8 Haydn String Quartet in B-flat Major, Op. 76, no. 4, "Sunrise," Finale.

In the following example from the first movement of Bartók's String Quartet No. 4, we explore a second method, using *Expressive Counting* to rehearse a thorny rhythmic passage by playing composite rhythms (see Figure 9.9).

120 The Art of Collaboration

FIGURE 9.9 Bartók String Quartet No. 4, Allegro, Boosey & Hawkes.

1. Observe the score and trace the imitative notes from one part to the next.
2. Without instruments, scat or use syllables to articulate the composite rhythm under tempo.
3. Once you feel comfortable speaking the composite rhythm together, play the passage in slow motion, with each member playing their part while listening for the composite rhythm.
4. Play the passage with a metronome at the indicated tempo.
5. Finally, play the passage without the metronome at the indicated tempo.

Understanding Syncopation

This technique can be helpful for working on or coaching groups struggling with syncopated passages. Technically, "syncopation occurs when a temporary displacement of the regular metrical accent occurs, causing the emphasis to shift from a strong accent to a weak accent."[9] For this technique, one ensemble member claps the strong beats and the other members clap the syncopated "off beats." Make sure everyone takes a turn to clap the strong beats and the syncopated off beats.

For example, measures 9–14 at the beginning of the *Presto* movement in Mozart's K. 157 quartet (see Figure 9.10) may pose a rhythmic challenge. By clapping the rhythms together—first slowly and then at the indicated tempo—you can literally

Techniques for Rhythmic Alignment and Ensemble   121

feel the syncopations in your body. Once you can clap the syncopations correctly with the strong beats, it will be easier to play them with your instruments.

FIGURE 9.10 Mozart String Quartet in C major, K. 157, Presto.

Left Hands Alone "à la Sasha Schneider"

> Play like you are eating up each other's left hands.
> ~ Alexander (Sasha) Schneider (Budapest String Quartet)

This technique unifies rhythm for string players through kinesthetic awareness. Donald Weilerstein of the Cleveland Quartet conceived (see Figure 9.11) *Left Hands Alone* as a means of connection invites you to focus on your colleagues and is a tactile way to establish the character of the music. Weilerstein describes the process as a sensation of emotional "electricity" moving through your entire body, your arm, and finally your fingers. As ensemble members articulate a passage without using bows, they watch each other's left hands with the goal of achieving simultaneous movement.

FIGURE 9.11 Donald Weilerstein, violinist. (Photo Credit: © Peter Schaaf)

This technique improves group relationships as every ensemble member must participate equally. The nonplaying, nonverbal aspect of sensing each other's left hands develops intimacy within the ensemble. This technique is not about slapping your fingers on the fingerboard. Instead, it is another way to conduct a musical gesture while focusing on connecting with your colleagues. These are the steps for practicing this technique:

1. Put down your bows. Select a passage that may be difficult to play together.
2. Begin with two people at a time.
3. Perform passage with left hands only, watching each other's left hands and sensing each other's fingertips.
4. Touch the instrument with a quality that reflects the character of the music, and touch the string, imagining the vibration as if you are touching a person.
5. Move from the back, elbow, hand, and fingers. The goal is to move together (fingers and whole body). Players lead and follow simultaneously.
6. Conduct the musical gesture through your left hand across to your colleagues.
7. **Ponticello**: Next, play the same passage with bows *ponticello*, listening for the high overtones. The overtones create a "tight knit" sound from the friction of high vibrations "rubbing together." Then play half *ponticello*, and finally with a slight *edge* in the sound (approximately 1/64 *ponticello*). This gives the feeling of "touching each other's sound by feeling the overtones."[10] See "Focus the Sound: Playing Ponticello" in the chapter "Techniques for Sound Production."

This technique takes commitment and hyperawareness among your collaborators. Everyone must lead with musical energy and in the character of the music.

Creating Rubato Through Agogic Playing

> The bottom line is that every note should have energy.
>
> ~ Karen Tuttle, Violist and Pedagogue

Like speaking or singing, playing an instrument communicates meaning through nuance and inflection. Drawing attention through *rubato* to the distinct shape of notes or phrases (e.g., beginning, middle, and end of the note or the duration or timing related to the adjacent notes) gives life to the music and communicates intention to the listener. *Rubato* refers to expressive and rhythmic freedom.

Understanding the emphasis implied by beat patterns is a first step in translating rhythmic nuance through music. Numerous scholarly sources and historical treatises are available to help understand the function of beat patterns and how they are interpreted throughout history. Take a look at The *Cambridge Companion to Rhythm* for a thorough overview.[11]

In addition, how and when you place emphasis or rhythmic timing on notes within a bar or a phrase can affect how the listener perceives the intent. This is called *agogic* playing, meaning "a variety of accentuation demanded by the nature of a particular musical phrase, rather than by the regular metric pulse of the music."[12]

An systematic approach to agogic playing was developed as *The Tabuteau Method* between 1925 and 1954 at The Curtis Institute by oboist Marcel Tabuteau. It involves breaking down phrases into their smallest components and rebuilding them using a numerical system.[13] In the system, each note of the phrase is assigned a number which reflects its relative intensity (1 represents the lowest level of intensity). The process reframes strong and weak beats so the player focuses on the overall shape and trajectory of the phrase rather than relying on bar lines as landing points.

For wind players, Tabuteau required that each musician "play the life of the note" by paying attention to the wind speed and not just intensity through volume. For string players, Tabuteau insisted that every note be shaped within the framework of the line and through a number of technical details—the relationship of the bow to the string and the touch of the left hand. Violist and pedagogue Karen Tuttle, who taught at the Curtis Institute was influenced by the musical ideals and method of Tabuteau and used his system in her teaching.

Agogic playing is a nuanced approach to interpreting and playing music through rhythmic emphasis. When playing in an ensemble, members must come to agreement regarding the placement of timing through expansion and contraction of a musical note or passage. Each member may demonstrate their agogic interpretation of a passage individually, and the ensemble can use the *LBAD* technique to play each interpretation together until arriving at a unified interpretation.

10
TECHNIQUES FOR INTONATION

In this chapter, we define intonation as the ability to hear and reproduce intervals *in tune*, meaning that each interval resonates within frequency ratios as identified by the ancient Greek philosopher Pythagoras. Good intonation enhances the quality of sound and resonance in performance. When interval relationships are understood and agreed upon, a group develops its own system of coherent and consistent tuning. When your group's intonation is aligned, the overtones generate a vibrant sound, and audiences respond to the natural resonance and beauty. In the rehearsal process, vigorous attention to intonation is another way to bond as an ensemble.

In This Chapter:

- Intonation Approach
- Warmup Routine with Intonation Techniques

Intonation Approach

> Regarding "intonation is biodegradable," I mean that intonation never stays. You always need to keep working on it. We don't have frets on the instrument. Intonation is something that's always there. It never gets to the point, "Oh now I play in tune." Regarding intonation, I say that a skunk can stand its own smell, but if you play out of tune, you may get used to it but no one else is going to like it.
>
> ~ Earl Carlyss, former member, Juilliard String Quartet

In This Section:
• Tuning Routine
• Tuning for String Ensembles
• Vertical Listening
• Melodic and Vertical Intonation

Intonation and sound production are intrinsically linked, as pure intonation creates a resonant sound. There is no scientifically perfect approach to intonation. Therefore, ensemble members must unite their approach to intonation as an essential aspect of the rehearsal process. A productive process for intonation work includes planned time during the rehearsal dedicated to intonation practice. An efficient tuning method offers ensembles a foundation for good intonation and a mindful routine to begin rehearsals.

The Art of Collaboration. Annie Fullard and Dorianne Cotter-Lockard, Oxford University Press. © Oxford University Press 2025.
DOI: 10.1093/oso/9780197673126.003.0011

FIGURE 10.1 Tuner. (Photo by Sandra Tenschert on Unsplash)

The two intonation systems most relevant to this chapter are *just intonation* and *equal temperament*. In just intonation, the intervals are calculated through Pythagorean mathematical relationships based on the natural overtone series. Equal temperament is a practical application of tuning that maintains perfect intervals (i.e., fourths, fifths, and octaves) in identical relationships to each other through all harmonies and is the current standard for tuning modern pianos and most instrumental ensembles. To learn more about the thought-provoking history and explanation of these two intonation systems, we recommend two books: *Temperament: How Music Became a Battleground for the Great Minds of Western Civilization* by Stuart Isacoff[1] and *How Equal Temperament Ruined Harmony (and Why You Should Care)* by Ross Duffin.[2]

Tuning Routine

It is essential to establish a tuning routine at the beginning of every rehearsal. We recommend using equal temperament and tuning to a tuner (see Figure 10.1). See the *Rehearsal Playbook* chapter for detailed guidance.

Tuning for String Ensembles

As one of the Cavani Quartet's formative coaches and mentors, Cleveland Quartet cellist Paul Katz offered profound musical and technical wisdom on the art of string quartet playing.[3] One of his most helpful techniques is a specific tuning process for string quartets—although it can be applied to all string ensembles—involving the following steps:

1. Each ensemble member tunes to a tuner one string at a time (adjust the tuner to equal temperament),[4] adjusting the fifths as needed (see Figure 10.1).

126   The Art of Collaboration

2. All ensemble members play together, testing one string at a time and adjusting as needed.
    a. Ensemble members play their A strings together
    b. Ensemble members play their D strings together
    c. Ensemble members play their G strings together
    d. The violist and cellist play their C strings together
    e. The violins play their E strings together
    f. Finally, play C strings at the same time as E strings to check for resonance and intonation. The E will sound a little sharp compared to the C, even with tempered tuning.
3. For larger string ensembles that include double bass, basses should check their E strings with the violins.

The Emerson String Quartet also recommends this process, and most professional string quartets follow a similar regimen. Tuning with a tuner has become the standard for most ensembles, and for string players, carefully tuning each string promotes better intonation.

Paul Katz recommends *CelloMind* by Jensen and Chung as a resource for practicing intonation that can be applied to string ensembles.[5] The *ViolinMind* book is also available.[6]

Vertical Listening

Intonation work during rehearsal highlights harmonic motion within the musical score and requires *vertical listening*. To develop vertical listening, build a chord from the bass note upward, tuning the chords individually. For example, in a string quartet, the cellist is often responsible for the bass line and establishes the foundation for resonant intonation. The inner voices (viola and second violin) often play the harmonies (e.g., the thirds and fifths in a chord). The first violinist often plays the melodic line, which may include octaves with the other parts. These roles sometimes switch, making it critical for ensemble members to be aware of the harmonic and melodic roles they are playing at any given time.

Next, listen for the *ring* or *resonance* as you build each chord vertically from the bass note up, caused by intervals that are in tune. We often use the term *resonant* sound because there is a mathematical and acoustic basis for *resonance*. The relationship of vibration frequencies explains why we hear a *ringing sound* or *resonance* when we play intervals that are in tune. Intervals and resonance are described in Box 10.1 below by composer, musicologist, and Pulitzer Prize winner Roger Sessions.[7]

To learn more about harmony and composition, we recommend reading *Elementary Training for Musicians* by Paul Hindemith[8] and The *Complete Musician: An Integrated Approach to Theory, Analysis, and Listening* (4th edition) by Steven G. Laitz.[9]

Box 10.1 A Note on Intervals—the Key to Great Intonation

According to Roger Sessions, "Any two tones which lie a fifth apart may be considered to be in the closest possible harmonic relationship." The first note of a scale is called the *tonic*, the fifth is called the *dominant*. Halfway between the tonic and dominant is the third, which is called the *mediant*. The term *interval* refers to the "relationship between two tones sounded simultaneously or in succession." Intervals are heard as a "musical sensation."

A Note on Resonance and Harmony

According to Roger Sessions, "Musical tones are produced by the regular vibration of 'sonorous bodies'; in most cases these latter are either columns of air, as in the case of the voice or the wind instruments, or taut strings, as in the case of the various types of stringed instrument. The detailed facts regarding the production of musical tone may be learned from any reference book on acoustical physics, and need not detain us here. The immediately relevant fact is that the vibration of a sonorous body produces, nearly always, not a single tone, but a whole complex of simultaneous tones called 'partials.'"

"There are partial tones because the sonorous body vibrates in a very complex manner—not only as a whole, but also, and simultaneously, in all of its fractions. Presumably every equal division ($\frac{1}{2}$, $\frac{1}{3}$, $\frac{1}{4}$, etc.) vibrates and produces at least a theoretical tone; and these tones contribute to the total effect of each musical sound."

Melodic and Vertical Intonation

Once your ensemble has developed the ability to hear and quickly adjust perfect intervals, the next step is to create a decision-making process for placing thirds, sixths, and sevenths within a chord. Since these interval relationships are more subjective, deciding where to place them can be based on either vertical harmony or a melodic framework. When approaching intonation from a vertical harmonic perspective, the ensemble may need to lower thirds and leading tones to relate the lines to the bass note. Likewise, a pedal or bass note may need to adjust based on harmonic progression.

When the ensemble approaches a passage using melodic intonation, the emotional context of the music dictates how the intervals will relate to each other. Melodic intonation generates tension and release through dissonance. Thirds and leading tones should be flexible to create resonance and emotional tension within the music.

Pitches may need to be adjusted slightly depending on whether they have a melodic or harmonic function and based on the key signature or modulation. The aim is to develop the ensemble's ability to adjust intonation in the moment to create a more expressive performance.

128   The Art of Collaboration

Warmup Routine with Intonation Techniques

No matter how long you've been together you always need to be attentive to honing your listening skills as an ensemble, not as individuals, but as an ensemble. If you get to the point when you assume that everyone is listening well, that's when things can go awry. As boring as it may be, play scales together and be certain that the overtones resonate.

~ Dr. Ronald Crutcher, cellist, President Emeritus,
University of Richmond

In This Section:

- Playing Scales
- Playing Bach Chorales
- Four-Tone Tuning
- Tuning Passages
- Listening Exercise: Tuning to a Drone
- Tuning as a Meditation

To achieve centered group intonation and pitch-accuracy, we recommend adding the following exercises to your warmup routine.

Playing Scales

Playing scales should be a foundational part of a warmup routine for individuals and ensembles. We designed the following exercises to help you take a mindful approach to playing scales. They are based on the diatonic scale system of the western European classical music tradition. The diatonic scale system is described in Chapter 4, and we recommend practicing scales from alternative tuning systems, including Asian, African, and Middle Eastern music.[10]

✓ Begin with a two-octave scale in unison or octaves at a moderate tempo. For string players, play one note per bow.
✓ Start by playing scales without *vibrato*. Playing without *vibrato* amplifies the resonance or ringing sound and helps you hear each pitch clearly.
✓ If a note sounds out of tune, say "back," and go back to that pitch.
✓ Focus on matching the sound quality.
✓ Learn to adjust notes quickly and agree on the placement of subjective intervals (e.g., thirds and sevenths).
✓ Cue yourselves in before you start the scale. This is a great opportunity to practice your cueing and breathing and play a beautiful scale together (see the chapter "Cueing and Breathing").
✓ Experiment with different dynamics.
  - For example, begin the exercise with everyone playing *piano* (string players: matching the contact point, speed, and pressure of the bow).
  - Next play the same scale *mezzo-piano*, next *mezzo-forte*, and finally *forte* and *fortissimo*.

Techniques for Intonation 129

✓ Add *vibrato* to the same scale, matching the speed and width of the *vibrato*.
✓ To increase your listening and responding skills, each member should take a turn initiating (cueing) the scale.

Variations

Once the routine of playing scales has become a natural part of your warmup routine, we encourage you to experiment with the following variations:

✓ Play the scale in chordal harmony. For example, in a string quartet, the first violin and cello would play in octaves, the viola would play the third of the scale, and the second violin would play the fifth of the scale.
✓ Invite each person to lead the scale with their choice of dramatic character, dynamics (e.g., adding *crescendos* and *decrescendos*), tempo, and varied articulations. The rest of the group matches the initiator. This may lead to laughter!

Playing Bach Chorales

> I start by helping students to learn how to listen, by using Bach chorales and scales.
>
> ~ Peter Salaff, former member, Cleveland String Quartet

Playing Bach chorales together is good for the soul. We found that playing chorales elevates and inspires the experience of working on intonation. There are more than 400 four-part Bach chorales in 24 keys. We recommend you choose one in the key of your repertoire. The original chorales or arrangements are available in the public domain (see Figure 10.2). The following steps will help refine your intonation as you play the chorales.

FIGURE 10.2 Bach Chorale, from David Bynog, "24 Chorale Harmonizations Transcribed for String Quartet," *Journal of the American Viola Society*.

130   The Art of Collaboration

✓ Begin without *vibrato* to achieve a pure, resonant sound.
✓ Match different styles of *vibrato* to achieve a consistent, blended sound throughout.
✓ Each ensemble member takes a turn initiating and cueing.
✓ Notice how it is necessary to widen the half step for chords.
✓ String players: Focus on matching bow speed, contact point, and pressure.
✓ Wacky Bach Chorales: Create your own Wacky Bach Chorale by experimenting with texture, sound production, tempo, *rubato*, and different dynamics.

Four-Tone Tuning Exercise

The cellist of the Cavani Quartet, Kyle Price, offers an exercise he learned from Les Thimmig, Professor of Saxophone at the University of Wisconsin-Madison. The four-tone tuning exercise is a great tool for ensembles of all levels. It helps members align their concept of group intonation in a kinetic and direct manner. Similar to how a composer may voice a major seventh chord across a quartet of instruments, each member plays a different part of a chord stack in this exercise.

✓ Each player plays either the root, third, fifth, or seventh, creating a major seventh chord.
✓ One at a time, each member changes their note by a half step, starting with the root. With each change, the nature of the chord shifts audibly and emotionally. This causes the player with the moving interval to find the ideal fit within the new-sounding chord.
✓ This is replicated by each member one by one in half steps, one octave up and down.
✓ When coming down, the order is reversed, starting with seventh, fifth, third, and root.

Focus on enjoying the sonorities and seek out a lush sound, colliding and mixing in the middle of the quartet, preferably without vibrato. For variation, feel free to have your ensemble rotate who plays root, third, fifth, or seventh and see how the chord shifts.

This can also be done in three-tone chords with the lowest and highest range instruments playing an octave relationship moving again in half steps. They move first, then the instrument with the fifth moves second (also up a half step), and then the final instrument moves the third interval up a half step to resolve the chord. This three-tone example is helpful when studying diatonic music, particularly from the western European musical canon.

Tuning Passages from Repertoire

This section includes approaches to tuning passages from the repertoire that are integral to the rehearsal process. They can be used as part of the warmup routine and at any time during the rehearsal.

In addition to *vertical listening*, it is critical to understand your role in relation to the other parts and within the musical texture. Roles might include melody, harmony, bass line, a drone, a rhythmic contrapuntal motive, or even an inventive sound effect. Each role requires balanced listening and active interpretation.

> **In This Section:**
>
> - Understanding Musical Texture
> - General Steps for Tuning Passages
> - Unison or Octave Passages
> - Chordal Passages

Understanding Musical Texture

Table 10.1 describes the most common types of musical textures in various compositions for ensembles. According to the *Sage Encyclopedia of Music and Culture*, "texture in music refers to the layers of sound in a piece of music and how those layers relate to one another."[11]

General Steps for Tuning Passages

Playing passages in slow motion while progressively adding voices, fine tunes the ear. This process expands our ability to interpret harmony and improve intonation and is an effective tool for equal participation. There is a difference between melodically conceived intonation and harmonically conceived intonation. Tempo significantly influences the perception of what makes a passage sound in tune. With music that moves at a fast pace, the ear is drawn to the melody. In slower tempos, adjust subjective intervals to the bass line rather than the melody (harmonically conceived intonation).

1. Begin by playing the passage in slow motion.
2. Start with two instruments at a time and add a new voice each time you play the passage.
3. Focus on resonance, blend, and matching *vibrato*. Become a virtuoso adjuster!
4. Balance the voices based on the role or function of your part (melodic, harmonic, baseline) based on the musical texture.
5. For wind players, Monica Ellis of Imani Winds advises using a tuner as a reference point for accurate intonation. This advice is also helpful to string players—use a tuner as a reference point for keys when you cannot use open strings.

Unison or Octave (Monophonic) Passages

Composers frequently write passages in unison or octaves to achieve an emphatic, spotlighted musical moment. This is an opportunity to demonstrate a virtuosic approach to intonation by achieving a unified, cohesive, and resonant sound.

1. When playing octaves, the upper voices should blend into the lower voice, and the lower voice should play louder than the upper voices to create resonance.

132   The Art of Collaboration

2. In an octave or unison passage, define how you approach intervallic relationships. Discuss half-step and whole-step interval relationships. For example, when using tempered intonation, the half steps will be wider and the whole steps will be narrower.

For string players who play the lower octave, the contact point of the bow should be closer to the bridge to produce a core sound, which enables easier adjustment by the other players.

Table 10.1 Musical textures.

Term	Definition
Monophony (unison)	One melody, played or sung by one or more instruments simultaneously, without accompaniment.
Homophony (chordal)	One melody supported by chords. This is the most common type of texture found in Western music. Homophonic music takes the form of a melody, harmony, and a bass line. Works by composers such as Mozart, Haydn, Mendelssohn, Schubert, and Brahms represent some of the most beautiful examples of homophony.
Polyphony (multiple melodies)	Two or more independent melodies or motives played simultaneously, for example, fugues by Bach, Mendelssohn, Beethoven, and other composer's contrapuntal music.
Melody and Drone	Melody and drone has its origins in the classical music of Central Asia, South Asia, the Middle East, eastern Europe, and North Africa. A drone effect occurs when one or more instruments play one or two sustained tones to support a melody. For example, we find this effect in the music of Bartók, Tan Dun, Lena Frank, and Shostakovich.
Polyrhythm	Polyrhythmic music includes layers of different rhythms performed simultaneously, and originates from Western African and Japanese drumming traditions. For example, John Cage wrote a piece called *Living Room Music*, which is a quartet for unspecified instruments using polyrhythm. Another example is *Breakfast at the Ibis* by Merry Peckham, which includes poetry, dundun (talking drum), and string quartet as part of our Collage: Music & Poetry program (https://cavanistringquartet.com/collage-music-poetry).
Call and Response	Call and response is a vocal performance form. A solo voice initiates a phrase that a group of singers or instrumentalists responds to in commentary or imitation. Call-and-response in music is expressed in a variety of religious and cultural contexts.

Chordal (Homophonic) Passages

Many ensembles spend a good part of their rehearsal time on focused intonation practice. This practice integrates with other aspects of the rehearsal process. We suggest using the list of musical textures in Table 10.1 as a reference to explore how the voices in the ensemble function and relate to the other parts.

1. Identify and tune all perfect intervals: fourths, fifths, and octaves.
2. Identify the bass line. The bass line is usually written in the lowest instrumental line, but not always.

3. Identify the melody in a chordal passage and balance it accordingly once you have tuned.
4. Decide how to approach the third of a chord. For instance, in a minor harmony, the third may be adjusted lower to achieve a darker quality.
5. Decide how to address the seventh scale degree. For expressive intonation, you may want the seventh to be higher. This is more applicable to a linear melodic line than to tuning a chord.
6. String players: Based on the harmony, use appropriate open strings as a reference.

A Listening Exercise: Tuning to a Drone

One of the most practical techniques for improving intonation and listening skills is to tune to a *drone*, a sustained note on a single pitch. Playing with a drone develops your capacity to hear and recognize intervals. This practice enhances the ability to make quick adjustments while playing a passage in real time. As a result, group members are entrained to naturally play in tune.

- ✓ One ensemble member holds a long drone note, while the other members play their intervals in relation to the drone pitch. The drone pitch in diatonic harmony can be the tonic, dominant, or another common tone which helps align the pitches in the passage.
- ✓ You may want to begin with one player at a time with the drone and then add in other group members.
- ✓ Match the dynamic and sound quality of the drone.
- ✓ A tuner can produce a drone sound; however, we recommend using the tuner for individual practice rather than in the group because a tuner does not produce the same resonance as an instrument.

Practicing with a drone encourages players to lower thirds and leading tones. It is important to note that this technique can work for some passages, but not others.

Tuning as a Meditation

In our experience, many ensembles perceive intonation work and the tuning process as frustrating, exhausting, or even a source of tension between players. Approach the process as a visual artist would, contemplating a palette of colors with which they might view the world. Enter the process meditatively, transcending the goal to play in tune. Enjoy the vibrations of the intervals and the resulting resonance, which affect your well-being. Through deep listening, we become aware of the sublime beauty of intervals and textures together as an ensemble, which is artistically transformative.

134   The Art of Collaboration

The application of mindfulness and meditative practices to music listening and performance continues to be a subject of study. A recent study conducted with music conservatory students who attended a course in mindfulness-based stress reduction (MBSR) revealed that during lessons, participants were able to focus more, let go of self-criticism, and increase body awareness, which resulted in improved learning. During individual practice, students felt that their creativity was enhanced, and their practice was more effective and efficient. The MBSR practices enhanced students' listening abilities and heightened collaboration during ensemble rehearsals.[12] Further resources related to MBSR practices can be found in Appendix A.

11

TECHNIQUES FOR SOUND PRODUCTION

Making a glorious sound together is one of the great joys of playing chamber music. Playing your instrument as if you are singing is fundamental for sound production. This chapter offers insight into vocal qualities for developing an expressive and nuanced sound and shares ideas for creating sound inspired by color and visual art. The chapter includes a section on articulation and producing a blended group sound and builds on the prior chapter on intonation. Finally, we offer sound production techniques on families of instruments based on interviews with noted chamber music performers and our experience.

In This Chapter:

- Achieving a Blended and Resonant Sound
- Vocal Inspiration
- Articulation and Diction
- Sound Production Techniques for Strings, Woodwinds, Brass, and Piano

Achieving a Blended and Resonant Sound

> How do you produce sound in reaction to the musical conversation you're having with other people?
>
> ~ Joel Krosnick, former member, Juilliard String Quartet

Regardless of the number of musicians in your ensemble, a *blended sound* results from unifying your approach. For a string quartet, a blended sound means that four voices become one by matching the use of the bow and left hand. For piano and string ensembles, the piano player can imagine that they are playing with a bow. In addition, string players should focus on the articulation and note length produced by the piano as a percussion instrument. For woodwind and brass players, the velocity and amount of wind used to produce sound should be carefully observed, along with the timbre.

Cultivate your ability to listen to the entire group to achieve a blended sound. In addition to developing acute listening skills, use visual connection, be aware of each player's physical technique for producing sound, and understand how a composer uses *tessitura*; the ranges or registers. Some parts may be in the same register or range and alternatively in contrasting registers. Register or *tessitura* may change throughout a piece or movement and affect the group sound.

The Art of Collaboration. Annie Fullard and Dorianne Cotter-Lockard, Oxford University Press. © Oxford University Press 2025. DOI: 10.1093/oso/9780197673126.003.0012

136 The Art of Collaboration

FIGURE 11.1 Mix of colors. (Photo by Joel Filipe on Unsplash)

Consider the image of mixing a vat of colors to create a blended sound (see Figure 11.1). Imagine each part as a different colored thread in a tapestry which intertwines to create the whole sound. The techniques in this chapter apply to larger string ensembles, brass, woodwind, and mixed ensembles.

Vocal Inspiration: Name That Singer

Listening to singers and emulating their approach to sound is a wonderful pathway to discovering your tonal color palette. Focus on how singers use vowel and consonant sounds and observe how they breathe to create phrasing and expression. For a chosen passage of chamber music, imagine the vocal quality of a particular singer who produces the sound quality you seek.

Find vocalists who inspire you—be creative with this process. For example, if you are a violinist, imagine the vocal personalities of Julie Andrews or Cecilia Bartoli for the E string, Beyoncé or Dawn Upshaw for the A string, and Whitney Houston or Ella Fitzgerald for the D and G strings. Brass players might emulate Mel Tormé's and Louis Armstrong's voices. Find singers from every genre of music whose vocal qualities you admire.

Apply Vocal Technique Concepts

In addition to the sound qualities of your favorite singers, instrumentalists can adapt and apply concepts related to vocal technique. The following are seven vocal techniques from the Fairfield County Children's Choir.[1] As you read them, you will notice parallels to the physical elements of playing an instrument.

1. Posture and alignment—centered and upright posture supports strong sound production.

Techniques for Sound Production **137**

2. Respiration—breathing motion (awareness of the body's movement while breathing) and breath management (awareness and control of the inhale and exhale).
3. Phonation and registers—conversion of air from the lungs, passing through the vocal folds of the air passageway and causing them to vibrate to produce sound.
4. Head or chest voice—the sound varies depending on how the air passes through the body.
5. Resonance—vowel sounds expand the range of resonance.
6. Articulation and diction—the sound production of vowels and consonants.
7. Expression—includes phrasing and dramatic communication of the text.

Articulation and Diction

Articulation and diction are vital to sound production. For instrumentalists, *diction* in vocal music links to articulation for instrumental players. Musical articulations function like punctuation in the spoken word to indicate expression, nuance, emphasis, and timing. This section explores a few of the most

> **In This Section:**
>
> - *Staccato*
> - *Legato*
> - Emphasis markings
> - *Vibrato*

common markings. Academic resources provide historically informed performance practice and information on the origins and meanings of articulation markings. You can deepen your knowledge using the resources in Appendix A. This section focuses on three basic types of articulation:

1. *Staccato*: dots (.) and wedges (▮)
2. *Legato*: slurs (▮) and phrase markings
3. Emphasis markings: accents (▮), *sforzando* (*sfz*), *fortepiano* (*fp*), and *tenuto* (▮)

Staccato: Dots and Wedges

Staccato originates from the word *detached* in Italian, and western European composers began using these common articulations around 1700. Consider staccato markings—dots or wedges—in the context of the musical style and genre and approach your interpretation with the spirit of discovery and with respect to the composer's musical language. Former first violinist of the Juilliard Quartet, Robert Mann, once said in response to playing dotted notes without intent, "Don't be hypnotized by the dots!" A *staccato* mark indicates more than a note of short duration—each should have a special character or emphasis, and players should have a variety of interpretive and instrumental tools to express *staccato*.

138 The Art of Collaboration

FIGURE 11.2 Laughter. Beethoven String Quartet in c minor, Op.18, No. 4, Scherzo

FIGURE 11.3 Sorrowful palpitations. Beethoven String Quartet in c minor, Op.18, No. 4, Scherzo

In rehearsal, sing or say the dotted notes in a way that reflects the character, dynamics, and phrasing. Use the singing technique to aid in making group decisions about the length, sound, and execution of *staccato* passages. For example, interpret *staccato* markings of composers such as Haydn, Mozart, and Beethoven with an operatic character. Experiment with singing the articulations with drama and flare as if you were an opera singer before you play them. In joyful passages, such as Beethoven's String Quartet Opus 18, No. 4 (see Figure 11.2), approach dotted notes as operatic laughter. In sections where dotted notes are under a slur, interpret them as *semi-legato*, to express quiet, sorrowful palpitations in a later passage of the same Beethoven quartet. In Figure 11.3, you can use the upper half or tip of the bow to create a soft and resonant dotted note. Interpret *staccato* notes by exploring a variety of possible lengths and articulations, even within a single movement.

In Gabriela Lena Frank's string quartet, *Leyendas: An Andean Walkabout*, you will find many articulation markings with both dots and wedges, invoking Lena Frank's interpretation of the folk music and songs of Peru (see Figure 11.4). Experiment with all different parts of the bow to achieve a variety of articulation and length.

FIGURE 11.4 Lena Frank, *Leyendas: An Andean Walkabout*, VI. Coqueteos, 2001.

Follow these steps to interpret dots and wedges:

1. Sing or say the passage of dotted notes before you play it.
2. Imitate that same articulation sound with your instrument.
3. Listen carefully to the end or release of the note and focus on releasing the ends of notes together.
4. Take turns cueing the end of the note or series of notes.

Mirror each other using the *LBAD* technique and explore different note lengths before making a final decision. Demonstrate an articulation for your colleagues and ask for feedback. Lastly, the decision regarding the note length will be influenced by the space where you rehearse and perform.

Legato: Slurs and Phrase Markings

Legato playing originates from vocal music, and it consists of more than playing a line smoothly. *Legato* (the Italian word for *tied-together*) markings should be interpreted

140 The Art of Collaboration

as an indication of the composer's phrasing to delineate musical shape and where to breathe within a line. It is essential to discuss dynamics, character, and style of music. Begin by trying the composer's original intention, however, consider slur markings as suggestions rather than an imperative.

Parlando (the Italian word for *speaking*) is another articulation in the *legato* family. It is often implied—but not always notated and is played by emphasizing certain notes under a slur for expressive purposes. This effect can be described as musical rhetoric (i.e., aligning musical patterns to speech), and relates to a style of singing and speaking simultaneously with a variety of inflections.[2] Famous twentieth-century violinist Fritz Kreisler was renowned for his *parlando* style of playing, drawing inspiration from singers of the time.

Singing together is an optimal way to rehearse a *legato* passage, and results in a free and natural sound. Romantic era composers who wrote *Leider* (songs), such as Johannes Brahms, Robert and Clara Schumann, Franz Schubert, and Felix and Fanny Mendelssohn, used *legato* markings to illuminate the musical gesture and rhetoric of their works. It is helpful to listen to the vocal works of these composers together as part of your rehearsal process.

Emphasis Markings—Sforzando, Fortepiano, Tenuto

Composers use numerous emphasis markings, and this section focuses on three of the most common notations. Each should be observed with deliberate attention to style, character, and dynamics. Every articulation marking should be approached as unique to the context in which it was written. This section includes guidelines relating to *sforzando*, *fortepiano*, and *tenuto*.

Sforzando (*sfz*)

Sforzando (*sfz*) is an indication to make a prominent, sudden accent on a note or chord. *Sforzando* translates from Italian, meaning "suddenly with force."[3] The effect is dramatic and compelling. At the dawn of romanticism, Beethoven frequently notated *sforzando*, one after another in sequence, to denote outbursts of tremendous emotion. The *sforzando* marking does not always mean to play *forte* (loud) but is an indication of intensity. When Beethoven begins in a soft dynamic such as *piano* or *pianissimo* with repeated *sforzandos*, the music expresses an insistent quality, implying an increasing dynamic level (see Figure 11.5). Beethoven's String Quartet, Opus 18 No. 1 features a series of *sforzandos* which grow dramatically from a soft dynamic (*pianissimo*) to *fortissimo* (see Figure 11.6).

Techniques for Sound Production   141

FIGURE 11.5 Progressive sforzandos. Beethoven String Quartet in F Major, Op.18, No. 1, Allegro con brio.

FIGURE 11.6 Sforzandos within a crescendo. Beethoven String Quartet in F Major, Op.18, No. 1, Allegro con brio.

Fortepiano (*fp*)

Fortepiano (*fp*) (strong and then immediately soft) is an expressive articulation marking commonly used during the late classical and early romantic musical eras. A *fortepiano* should not sound the same as *sforzando*—it implies added emphasis that gives more weight to a certain note in the measure. In many instances, *fortepiano* denotes a slight hold or expressive timing to fully achieve the composer's intent. The *fortepiano* marking is frequently found in the works of Mozart and could be interpreted as a "speed bump." This articulation is best practiced by singing the passage first and imitating the sound on your instrument.

142 The Art of Collaboration

Tenuto (⊖)

Tenuto means *to hold* in Italian and indicates sustaining a note for a slightly longer duration than it is written. *Tenuto* markings are frequently found under a slur and should be played by barely releasing the note before moving to the next. Imagine feeling an expressive pull from note to note.

Articulations—General Guidance

Here is some final guidance:

- ✓ Play the passage without the articulation markings. This highlights the absence of articulations, allowing discovery of the composer's intention when you reintroduce them.
- ✓ Assign descriptive words to illustrate the sound you wish to achieve as a group. Descriptions such as *brooding* or *mysterious* unify the ensemble's approach to sound production and can alleviate protracted arguments about technical details.
- ✓ Remain open in the discussion to a variety of ideas and solutions (see *Try Every Idea* in Chapter 2).

Vibrato: To Vibrate or Not to Vibrate

> So many students have what I call a "doorbell" vibrato. It's always the same speed. Listen to any slow movement of Jasha Heifetz and listen to the variety of vibratos that he uses, and how that changes the personality of the sound. If you have the flexibility to control different speeds of vibrato and control the three basic colors of the bow arm, it expands the whole musical world enormously.
>
> ~ Earl Carlyss, former member, Juilliard String Quartet

Vibrato is a resource for creative expression which requires mindful application to the character of the music. Rather than being an automatic function of playing the instrument, it is best to use it intentionally. To determine the choice of *vibrato*, research the style and trends of the composer's era. The following guidelines will help develop your interpretation and application of *vibrato*.

- ✓ Practice scales with constant *vibrato* as well as *senza vibrato*. Practice varying the amplitude and velocity.
- ✓ Choose the velocity (speed) and amplitude (width) that best expresses the character of the music. For example, slow and wide *vibrato* can give a rich, expressive sound, while fast and narrow *vibrato* can evoke an ecstatic and glowing quality.

Techniques for Sound Production **143**

✓ Try different combinations of speed and amplitude depending on the passage.
✓ Be intentional about your use of *vibrato*. If a passage requires expressive *vibrato*, ensure you vibrate continuously from note to note.
✓ Consider imitating the human singing voice.

String Instrument Techniques for Sound Production

> If you think of the three primary colors, they are red, blue, and yellow. With the bow arm, you have three primary colors: you have the pressure into the string, you have the speed of the bow, and you have the position on the string between the fingerboard and the bridge. Once the bow is on the string, all colors are a combination of those three elements.
>
> ~ Earl Carlyss, former member, Juilliard String Quartet

This section offers techniques for producing colors with the bow and left hand. The primary aim is to envision your bow and left hand as artistic tools for deeper expression.

In This Section:

- The Bow
- Vibrato Techniques
- Kinesthetic Sound Production

The Bow

> If you need a more mysterious sound then you need to play with a weaker contact point and a little more bow.
>
> ~ Joel Krosnick, former member, Juilliard String Quartet

String players use the following four aspects of bow technique: contact point, bow speed, pressure, and angle of bow hair. Consider the bow as a paint brush and choose a combination of these four aspects to emulate the voice and to create color. Based on the composer's intent, a string ensemble might choose a *colorless sound* to express a certain quality of emotion by floating the bow over the fingerboard with a slow bow speed and no *vibrato*. In another passage, they might choose a warm, glowing sound by playing closer to the bridge with faster bow speed and a fast, narrow *vibrato*.

The following aspects are highlighted in detail in Appendix D, "Sound Production Techniques for Strings: The Bow":

✓ Organizing bowings
✓ Technique to practice bow use (bow speed, pressure, contact point, bow angle)
✓ Legato bowings
✓ Emphasis markings (*staccato* and *sforzando*)

Vibrato Technique

Resources are available which describe the use of *vibrato* as it applies to string playing and interpretation (see Appendix A). For example, string instrumental music of the European Medieval and Renaissance periods use the bow for expression rather than *vibrato*. The study of the origins of the bow and string instruments is fascinating—it deepens our understanding of sound production and the use of *vibrato*.

Many performers specialize in the study of early European music. Olivier Brault, Canadian violinist and member of The Four Nations Ensemble and Apollo's Fire, specializes in the Baroque and Classical repertoire (see Appendix A). Seek recordings and information about the history of string instruments.

An intriguing reference to eighteenth-century style and string technique is *A Treatise on the Fundamentals of Violin Playing* by Leopold Mozart, Wolfgang Mozart's father.[4] Leopold Mozart refers to *vibrato* as *tremolo*. He describes it as follows:

> *Tremolo* is an ornamentation which arises from Nature herself and which can be used charmingly on a long note, not only by good instrumentalists but also by clever singers. Nature herself is the instructress thereof. For if we strike a slack string or a bell sharply, we hear after the stroke a certain wave-like undulation of the struck note. And this trembling after-sound is called *tremolo*, also *tremulant* [or *tremoleto*]. (Leopold Mozart)

In twentieth- and twenty-first-century compositions, a non-*vibrato* approach can be appropriate to express the character for certain passages. For example, in the expository section of Shostakovich's Quartet No. 8, the composer does not indicate *senza vibrato*, but the drone sound of the open strings and the desolate quality of the music imply a less expressive approach to the left hand.

Match *vibrato* in combination with matching bow speed once you have determined the character and tempo and organized bowings for a particular section of the music.

Kinesthetic Sound Production Techniques

> Touch the instrument as you want it to sound. . . . Players produce sound from their bodies into their left hand, by singing through their bodies, through their arms, and then into their hands. If they sing through their bodies that way, they can establish a kind of rapport and can sense each other's touch on the string.
>
> ~ Donald Weilerstein, former member, Cleveland String Quartet

Violinist and former member of the Cleveland Quartet, Donald Weilerstein, is widely respected for his approach to creating expressive sound through physical sensitivity. He uses a kinesthetic approach to right- and left-hand technique. *Kinesthetic* means an awareness of the position and movement of the body. In this section, we expand on his sound production techniques for connecting right and left hands and playing *ponticello*.

Kinesthetic Approach—Connect Right and Left Hands

Apply kinesthetic learning by focusing on how your hands, arms, and fingertips feel when you play your instrument. Weilerstein suggests that the touch you use on the fingerboard in combination with your bow stroke influences your sound production. He often encourages students to feel the vibration of the strings coming up from fingers into fingertips.

The way you touch your instrument translates to the musical expression you project to your group members and the audience. This sensory method significantly impacts one's approach to playing and can transform how you produce sound in an expressive way.

The following strategies develop kinesthetic awareness:

✓ Consider how much of the finger pad to use depending on the character of the passage. A slow, singing, expressive passage would call for more of the fleshy part of the finger to be in contact with the string. In a fast, virtuosic passage, use the fingertips to rebound vigorously off the fingerboard.
✓ Focus on how left and right hands work together to produce sound by connecting distinct fingers from both hands simultaneously. For example, connect the third finger on the bow with the third finger of the left hand.
✓ Think of a desired sound quality and consciously produce the sound by visualizing a connection between right and left hands.
✓ Try this technique progressively with each finger.

Focus the Sound: Playing Ponticello

Have students play ponticello, which gives them a feeling of the high overtones . . . it gives a feeling of playing into the vibrations, and they can get a blended sound but also with a lot of friction. They can feel how the sounds rub against each other.

~ Donald Weilerstein, former member, Cleveland String Quartet

Ponticello helps produce a more resonant sound by producing high overtones, even in *piano* passages. Donald Weilerstein developed this technique to help students, and it is used for both individual and ensemble sound production. The technique empowers string players to generate a bigger sound by observing the placement of the bow in relation to the bridge.

Weilerstein often uses this technique to unify an approach to sound quality within a passage. Playing *ponticello* modifies the sound and attunes players to each other. The result generates deeper character in an ensemble's sound. Follow these steps to apply the *ponticello* technique.

1. Choose a passage: select a passage which poses a challenge to the group for sound quality and balance.
2. Play the passage *ponticello*, listening for the high overtones. The overtones create a "tight knit" sound from the friction of high vibrations "rubbing together." Each player commits to playing as close as possible to the bridge—this may sound strange the first time you try it.
3. Play half *ponticello*. This gives the feeling of "touching each other's sound by feeling the overtones."
4. Repeat the passage: progressively move the bow further away from the bridge each time, and finally with a slight *edge* in the sound (approximately 1/64 *ponticello*).
5. Focus on the contact point: carefully listen to the overall group sound, paying attention to producing a ringing, core sound.
6. Finally, play the passage without *ponticello*: the group will find that the sound is fuller and more resonant.

Woodwind and Brass Techniques for Sound Production

According to Monica Ellis, founder of Imani Winds and Jeff Scott, former member, Imani Winds, it is essential to learn how each instrument in a wind ensemble produces sound. The first step is to learn about the embouchure for each instrument, how much wind is used to make their sound, and how articulations are made. According to Scott, since pedagogy is unique across different instruments, people learn how to breathe in different ways. What is efficient for one instrument may be less efficient for another. Therefore, it is important to breathe together so the ensemble plays together.

In addition, Ellis suggests recognizing the connection of the breath along with the engagement of the diaphragm, abdomen, and lower back muscles. All these elements go into the unique production of sound for each instrument. Observe what it takes for each person to create their sound. Having this awareness helps understand what you need to do with your instrument to play together.

Each wind instrument has a different timbre. Sometimes you will highlight the differences, depending on the musical context. Other times, the music calls for a blended sound. The decision is guided by the composer's notation and your group's interpretation. Ellis explained that one way to create different colors is to *dig* or *go into* each other's sound. For example, you may want the French horn to be more prominent, even if you are playing in unison or in harmony. You can achieve this by allowing the French horn to dictate the timbre and then match their sound quality.

Finally, practice chord building to achieve balance by following these steps, which can also be applied as an intonation exercise:

1. Start with a major triad—some notes will be doubled since there are five players.
2. Build from the bass note up (usually the bassoon and French horn play the bass)
3. Try a series of chord changes, adjusting to a minor triad, and returning to major.
4. Try playing a diminished or an augmented chord, and then go back to major.
5. Change your roles in the chord (the bassoon can play the third or the fifth of the chord rather than the bass note).
6. Match your sounds and find an equal balance.

Piano Techniques for Sound Production

> I try not to sound like a "piano," ever. . . . My teachers always encouraged to emulate fine singers or instruments of the orchestra, using as a large a color palette as possible.
> ~ Anton Nel, pianist, Head of the Division of Keyboard Studies,
> Butler School of Music, University of Texas at Austin

A wide variety of sublime piano chamber music is available for study and performance. As we approach the acoustical properties of an ensemble that combines the piano with other instruments, there are important elements to consider. The piano is part of the percussion family and uses a complicated system of mechanics to produce sound. Detailed information about the mechanics and history of the piano are widely available (see resources in Appendix A).

148 The Art of Collaboration

> **In This Section:**
>
> - Listening, Balance, and Sound Palette
> - Piano Techniques for Controlling Dynamics
> - Touch and Response

All players need to be acutely sensitive in listening for balance, timbre, and articulation in relation to the piano. Our conversations with renowned pianists and collaborators Anton Nel and Vivian Hornik Weilerstein highlight essential aspects of playing piano chamber music, which we include in the following section.

Listening, Balance, and Sound Palette

> As a pianist, I love the sound of piano and strings together. The blending between the piano and strings, coloration of harmony, textural aspects, and the combination of the registration between piano and strings all contribute to the beauty of the combined sound. The piano provides ring and can absorb vibrato into the piano sound. The harmony from the piano can envelop/surround the string sound.
>
> ~ Vivian Hornik Weilerstein, pianist, Director Professional
> Piano Trio Program, piano and collaborative piano faculty,
> New England Conservatory of Music

A pianist's approach to listening is informed by understanding the score and how their part relates to other members of the ensemble. It is vital for pianists to recognize the musical and sonic roles they play in any ensemble. Balance and voicing in piano chamber music is inspired by the style and character of the music. For example, in the Schumann piano quintet, the pianist adjusts the balance accordingly when their part doubles another (see Figure 11.7). In cases where the piano plays in unison or doubles the line, the pianist should illuminate the sound of the other instrument. In addition, pianists need to recognize when they serve as a sonic foundation or have a melodic line which needs to be more prominent. The experience of listening and creating music in an ensemble provides pianists an avenue for adopting a variety of roles, whether soloistic, supportive, blending, enhancing, or a steering role.

Piano Techniques for Controlling Dynamics

> Pedaling is a whole art unto itself.
> ~ Anton Nel, pianist, Head of the Division of Keyboard Studies,
> Butler School of Music, University of Texas at Austin

Anton Nel suggests that pianists approach dynamics differently based on whether they are playing solo recitals, concerti, or chamber music. For example, when playing

FIGURE 11.7 Schumann Piano Quintet in E-flat Major, Op.44, Allegro brillante.

a solo piece that includes a *fortissimo*, a pianist will play with the loudest sound possible. However, in chamber music, one should interpret *fortissimo* depending on the musical and acoustic context of the ensemble. Ensemble members need to be aware of the cumulative sound to ensure the balance illuminates the most prominent line.

150   The Art of Collaboration

Pianists should develop a different palette of sounds for each genre. Pedal use and placement of the piano lid influence the variety of sounds a piano can produce. Anton Nel suggests that the difference between half- and full-stick relates to resonance. The pianist must listen carefully and adjust their volume based on the piano resonance, the balance with other instruments, and the room acoustics. It is vital to cultivate these skills when changing between half- and full-stick in piano chamber music. Playing with the full-stick while adjusting for balance ensures maximum resonance.

In addition, by using the pedal effectively, pianists can create a halo of sound that can carry the ensemble, especially in a space with dry acoustics. Pedal use will vary based on acoustics and instrumentation and should reflect the musical meaning and character. For example, in a drier acoustic, use more pedal and use less in a live acoustic.

Touch and Response

> One of the things that I think is key for a pianist, is to be able to sense the bow. That is a very specific technical/musical concept where a pianist really needs to sense and feel the point of contact between the bow hair and the string. Once a pianist is sensitized to that, it changes the entire world of ensemble between the piano and strings. It becomes a much more unified and integrated ensemble.
>
> ~ Vivian Hornik Weilerstein, pianist, Director Professional Piano
> Trio Training Program, New England Conservatory of Music

A pianist produces sound through the touch and the release of their fingers on the keyboard. When a piano key is depressed, the note sounds instantaneously, which differs from the sound produced by string or wind instruments. String players produce sound when the bow causes the string to resonate, and wind players rely on air moving through their instruments. It is necessary to anticipate potential timing differences for sound initiation. Pianists should imagine they are playing with a bow or breathing like a singer or wind player. In piano chamber music, ensemble members should listen for the beginning and endings of notes since the piano does not sustain notes the same way as string, woodwind, or brass instruments.

12

TECHNIQUES FOR PROJECTING EXPRESSION

> When we perform, we are describing a piece in the air in the room, moving sound from the stage to the people for whom we are playing.
>
> ~ Joel Krosnick, former member, Juilliard String Quartet

In This Chapter:

- Singing
- Standing
- Expressing Dynamics
- Playing to the Center
- Playing by Memory

The techniques in this chapter will help ensembles develop their unique voice as an expressive unit. These techniques for projecting expression also help develop a collaborative working environment, making rehearsals more productive and joyful. One of the great joys of playing chamber music occurs when a group plays with one mind and heart (see Figure 12.1).

Singing

> The only thing better than singing is more singing
>
> ~ Ella Fitzgerald

This technique builds on the concepts introduced in the prior chapter related to vocal inspiration. Singing is most helpful when your ensemble feels stuck in the rehearsal process regarding projecting phrasing, nuance, and character. Singing parts together helps engage members in a musical conversation. By removing the focus from the technical aspects of playing an instrument, singing frees the expression of the sound and helps illuminate the group's interpretation of the music. Singing your parts helps understand the character and balances the blend and quality of sound. Singing can also illuminate solutions to technical challenges with your instrument.

✓ Choose a passage of music which poses a challenge to phrasing, nuance, or character.

The Art of Collaboration. Annie Fullard and Dorianne Cotter-Lockard, Oxford University Press. © Oxford University Press 2025.
DOI: 10.1093/oso/9780197673126.003.0013

152   The Art of Collaboration

FIGURE 12.1 Students from Encore String Quartet Intensive.

- ✓ Be courageous, as this technique does not require professional vocal skills.
- ✓ Use your natural voice to express musical ideas.
- ✓ Participate without judgment.
- ✓ Do your best to match the pitches written in your parts.
- ✓ Express all articulations and dynamics in the score through singing.
- ✓ Add words or syllables that go with the music and are appropriate to the style of the composer.

If you are coaching students who are self-conscious about singing, become a role model. It is empowering for the teacher or coach to sing with students with expression and in full character, so they do not feel self-conscious.

Throw caution to the wind—do not worry about the sound or intonation—it is common to have a limited range of notes if you have not studied voice. If you are working on a work by Mozart, you may sing in an operatic style. For Schubert, you might want to sing as if it is poetry from an art song (*lieder*). If you know the native language of the composer, you can use words in their language.

Chamber Works Inspired by Song

Singing is one of the earliest forms of human expression. By practicing the technique of singing our parts, we create new relationships between instrumental music and song. Romantic era composers frequently linked their instrumental works to songs (*Lieder*). Figure 12.2 illustrates the beginning of the song (*Lied*), *Die Forelle*, written by Franz Schubert. He later used the theme from this song for the 4th movement of the Piano Quintet in A Major, *Die Forelle*, *"The Trout"* (see Figure 12.3). This example illustrates a direct relationship between a song and instrumental music.

Techniques for Projecting Expression   153

FIGURE 12.2 "Die Forelle," Op.32, D. 550, Franz Schubert, 1817.

FIGURE 12.3 Schubert Quintet in A Major, Op.114, D. 667, "The Trout," Tema con variazione, Andantino, 1819.

In Charles Washington's string quartet *Midnight Child* (1987), the composer incorporates the melody from a spiritual, "Sometimes I Feel Like a Motherless Child," which became widely recognized when the Fisk Jubilee Singers performed it in the 1870s.[1] Washington set the tone of the piece with a mournful violin solo based on the spiritual. After the opening measures, the entire quartet joins to play the melody, creating a beautiful harmonic landscape. He further developed the theme from the spiritual into a twelve-bar blues solo for each quartet member. This piece is one of the Cavani Quartet's favorites because it is so deeply expressive.[2]

Scat Singing

> I invite students to show me how they would shape the phrase with their hand while singing or scatting. Everyone stands up and sings or scats the line. Each person passes the line to the next person with hand gestures.
> ~ Peter Salaff, former member, Cleveland String Quartet

Scat singing is the use of nonsense syllables when engaged in vocal improvisation in jazz music.[3] Scat singing first emerged in the American jazz scene in the early twentieth century and was popularized by Louis Armstrong and Ella Fitzgerald. The

154 The Art of Collaboration

Cavani Quartet adapted the concept of scat singing in rehearsal as inspired by our mentor Peter Salaff. This technique is highly effective for complicated rhythms and phrasing. It is beneficial for group members who are uncomfortable with singing.

- ✓ If you are not familiar with scat singing, listen to videos or recordings of Ella Fitzgerald.[4]
- ✓ Try "scat speaking" or scat singing a short section, using a syllable such as *da*, *la*, or another syllable of your choice that portrays the character of the passage.

Begin with one line of a simple rhythm, such as the opening to Joseph Bologne, Chevalier de St. George's Quartet Op. 1, No. 4, *Rondeau* movement (see Figure 12.4). Each member of the ensemble scats their line. Begin with two voices at a time and progressively add another until all voices speak together.

FIGURE 12.4 Joseph Bologne, Chevalier de St. George, String Quartet in g minor, Op.1, No. 4, Rondeau. (Score realized from parts by David Wolfson)

In a more complicated example, Bartók's String Quartet No. 4, *Allegro* (see Figure 12.5) poses rhythmic and expressive challenges in the opening composite rhythm (see "Playing Composite Rhythms" in the chapter "Techniques for Rhythmic Alignment and Ensemble"). Scatting the parts rather than counting the rhythms helps to understand the rhythmic relationships and expressive nuance.

FIGURE 12.5 Bartók String Quartet No. 4, Allegro.

Standing

In This Section:
• Stand and Play
• Stand and Walk

Standing as a rehearsal technique is one of the best ways to increase projection and energize the group's sonic presence. It can help you develop a different awareness of your fellow group members and inspires players to communicate more freely across space. Players who are unable to stand can imagine the sensation of standing while playing. Standing can be thought of as a metaphor to represent an open and upward posture of the body along with expression from the body's center.

Stand and Play

Playing while standing frees the body and creates greater resonance in the ensemble. In addition, standing assists in projecting sound beyond the space of the ensemble (see Figure 12.6). Use the following tips for practicing this technique:

- Play a passage standing up: Be mindful of generating the sound from your entire body—focus on leading from your back and legs.
- Cello players: Consider trying the Block Strap, designed by Mike Block, which allows cellists to play standing up (https://www.cellostrap.com).
- Incorporate *Chamber Music Aerobics* (see the chapter "Rhythmic Alignment and Ensemble"). March in place or sway in time to the music while playing.
- Take turns standing up when you have the theme and sitting down when you do not.
- When there's a *crescendo*, group members can rise from their seats to physically demonstrate the feeling of getting louder. Alternately, lower yourself to a seated position during a *decrescendo*.
- While standing: Take turns directing your sound by leaning toward different group members while you play.
- Project the sound outward from the center of the group toward an imagined audience while standing:
  1. Imagine a circle drawn on the floor around each member.
  2. Expand the imaginary circle to include everyone in the ensemble while playing the passage.
  3. Expand the circle to an imaginary audience while playing the passage.
  4. Expand the circle to the furthest corners of the space.

156 The Art of Collaboration

FIGURE 12.6 Stand and play. Students at Robert McDuffie Center for Strings, Mercer University.

Stand and Walk

This technique helps develop relationships based on listening, sensing, and projecting energy between performers and the audience. Ensemble members exaggerate the space between them to project drama and energy. The objective is to heighten awareness and connection between members of the ensemble. This technique is useful when two or more ensemble members are having difficulty connecting rhythmically or sonically. Practice the following steps:

1. Begin with two ensemble members who have simultaneous rhythms or lines in counterpoint.
2. Ensemble members stand far apart in the corners of the room. Begin playing while walking toward each other at a natural pace.
3. Establish eye contact. Direct the sound, musical intention, and physical energy across the room to each other.
4. Exaggerate the effort to reach out and connect across space through *tempo* and body language.
5. Add other group members as needed to coalesce the rhythm and sound.

Expressing Dynamics

In This Section:

- Practicing Dynamics
- Playing the Silences
- Creating Your Dynamic Chart

Dynamics express the volume and inflection of notes within a passage—they are intrinsic to the language of music. Composers use dynamic notations to represent an emotional landscape that communicates powerful intensity in loud and soft passages.

In chamber music playing, it is vital to project character in addition to sound volume. Ensemble members should be fully attentive to the dynamics in their part and aware of how those relate to the group sound. An ensemble that creates a breathtakingly soft sound will leave an audience spellbound—likewise, an ensemble that projects the emotional force of climactic moments can move an audience to tears. The overall effect of dynamic contrast and nuance can be magical. This section offers guidance on projecting the character of dynamics.

Practicing Dynamics Together

Once you have examined the dynamics through score study, practice expressing dynamics as an ensemble. Practicing dynamics develops active listening skills. Focus on matching volume through sound quality and become aware of instrumental timbre, range, and color. The following steps will help you develop a dynamic sound palette.

1. Play a one-octave scale together ensuring you are matching sound (first in *pianissimo*, next in *piano*, followed by *mezzo-piano*, and so on until you play the scale *fortissimo*).
2. Play a one-octave scale with tiered dynamics so the group creates a natural *crescendo*, beginning with *pianissimo*, moving up the scale, and a *decrescendo* from *fortissimo* moving down the scale.
3. Each ensemble member leads the scale with a different dynamic scheme (see the chapter "The Capstone Technique: Live, Breathe, and Die").

Practice expressing the emotional character of dynamics to unify the interpretive approach. Explore the characters necessary to bring the composer's dynamic indications to life. Examples of character descriptions include frustration, tragedy, loneliness, consolation, tenderness, triumph, and joy (see Appendix B for a comprehensive list of descriptive words).

158   The Art of Collaboration

✓ Choose a phrase or passage from your repertoire. Discuss the dynamic character, then write descriptive words into your part to guide your technical approach to producing the indicated dynamics.
✓ Sing or scat the passage to interpret the dynamic character. Try a whisper for *pianissimo* (***pp***) and a shout for *fortissimo* (***ff***).
✓ Try playing a soft passage *fortissimo* and a loud passage *pianissimo*.

   Observe all emphasis markings notated within a dynamic marking, such as an accent (▤), *sforzando* (***sfz***), and *fortepiano* (***fp***). These notations will have different functions depending on the composer's context. For further guidance, refer to the chapter "Techniques for Sound Production."

Playing the Silences

Silence is a dramatic musical element. Once you have studied the score and circled all silences in your part, the ensemble can practice the silences together. Peter Oundjian, former member, Tokyo String Quartet, and conductor emeritus of the Toronto Symphony Orchestra, advises students in a particularly dramatic moment to "play the silence with an accent."

✓ Play the silence at the end of a phrase or during a rest by holding the character of the music. Like great theater actors, silence can be held in the posture of our bodies to demonstrate drama and character.
✓ Hold the dynamic and mood at the end of a piece. Many works end with a *fermata* over a rest (▤), which indicates a heightened dramatic moment. Allow a moment of silence to frame the movement.
✓ Remain still (freeze) during the silence at the end of a movement. For string players, use the bow to indicate the mood at the end of a movement or phrase. You can use what the Cavani Quartet has lovingly named "the armpit," with bows fully raised above our heads (see Figure 12.7).

Creating Your Dynamic Chart

The Cavani Quartet uses the following table as a starting point to interpret dynamics. Our former cellist, Merry Peckham, assigned descriptive words to each dynamic marking to facilitate our interpretive process. Juilliard String Quartet former member Robert Mann spoke at length about the development and use of dynamics from the eighteenth century—we incorporated his ideas in Table 12.1. We encourage you to discover the emotional landscape inspired by the dynamics. Try using the descriptive words in the table and then create your own.

Techniques for Projecting Expression   159

FIGURE 12.7 "The Armpit" during final note of Dvořák "American" Quartet in F Major, Op. 96. (Photo credit: Stephen Wolfe)

Table 12.1 Cavani Quartet's dynamic chart

Dynamic	Interpretation
Pianissimo	1) Distant 2) Suppressed energy 3) Intimate
Piano	Singing or speaking voice
Mezzo piano	Aware
Mezzo forte	Confident
Forte	*Forte* is an attitude—*Forte* means strong, proud, noble—not necessarily just "loud."
Fortissimo	*Everything you've got!*

The late Robert Mann shared a story with Cavani Quartet members during a coaching session to help understand the power of dynamics to express character. The story was about Beethoven conducting his own Symphony No. 5 in front of the orchestra during a rehearsal. Beethoven jumped on and off the podium to embody the soft and loud dynamics, inspiring the orchestra to express sudden dynamic changes in the score.

In *Absolutely on Music: Conversations with Seiji Ozawa*, Haruki Murakami offered Robert Mann's thoughts on dynamics. The following passage relates the wisdom from Robert Mann, as recounted by Murakami and Ozawa:[5]

160 The Art of Collaboration

Murakami: Another thing that Robert Mann mentioned frequently was that the instruction to play *piano* doesn't mean to play weakly. Any number of times I heard him say, "*Piano* means half as strong as *forte*, so play at a lower volume but play with *strength.*"

Ozawa: He's right about that. When we see *piano* in a score, we tend to soften everything up, but what he's saying is, even if the volume is lower, make those notes clearly audible. Give even the weaker sounds their proper rhythm and emotional force. Balance tension and release. He has gained this faith from over half a century of playing string quartets.

Playing to the Center

Playing to the Center is fundamental to expanding group projection and expression. This practice was inspired by Peter Salaff, who encourages students to visualize a physical center or sphere of energy in the middle of the ensemble. This technique helps strengthen connection and teaches ensemble members how to direct and focus energy during performances.

1. Imagine that there is a sphere of energy in the center of the ensemble.
2. Play a passage while directing your energy to the center.
3. *"Be Up"*: Concentrate your visual focus up and across the group beyond the music stands.
4. While playing, group members lean toward the center.
5. Finally, imagine you are directing the energy from the center of the group outward toward the audience.

This technique enables the ensemble to project in a large space—imagine projecting your sound and energy to the last row or the back of the hall. It is also helpful to visualize sending the energy to a specific person who is in the audience.

Playing by Memory

The challenge of committing to play by heart and getting to know the dynamics, the chords, and the notes intimately, allowed us to be more connected with each other and to play with freedom. We were looking for spontaneity—it was a riveting experience
~ Hyeyung Sol Yoon, member, Del Sol Quartet,
former member Chiara String Quartet

Playing by memory enables complete expressive freedom and connection between members. The intention is not to play entire works from memory but to experience

Techniques for Projecting Expression   161

FIGURE 12.8 Cavani Quartet rehearsing by memory. (Photo credit: Robert Muller)

the freedom of playing short passages without music in front of you. Group members can freely communicate across the ensemble by removing physical barriers such as music stands and visual dependence on printed notes (see Figure 12.8).

Practicing small sections by memory, such as the opening or ending of a movement, can improve the ability to play with more energy and commitment.

- ✓ Remove the music stands and sit or stand as close together as possible.
- ✓ Play a small excerpt from memory—for example, the opening or final measures of a piece.
- ✓ Become aware of the sonic and emotional connection between the group members.

Playing by memory allows us to pay attention to our physical senses. Our mentors in the Cleveland Quartet taught us to form a musical connection by sensing and listening for the vibrations between instruments. You can sense the vibration related to dissonance as it resolves to consonance. In addition, you can sense the vibrations between supportive and melodic lines. Playing by memory while sensing vibrations expands your ability to be an expressive collaborator.

13

TECHNIQUES FOR STRATEGIC LISTENING AND BALANCE

The techniques in this chapter focus on improving and deepening musical listening skills. *Strategic listening* is the ability to highlight different musical lines. These techniques aid in the production of a resonant, well-balanced, integrated sound.

A fundamental challenge of playing chamber music is to achieve an appropriate balance based on the score. Score study reveals the roles of each voice at each point in the piece. It is every member's responsibility to find a balance for any given passage. These techniques are valuable for larger conductor-less ensembles, such as a small chamber orchestra. This chapter contains several techniques to enhance your attention and listening skills.

In This Chapter:

- Shining the Light
- The Listening Game
- Switching Seats
- Playing with Backs to Each Other

Shining the Light

Peter Salaff introduced this technique to the Cavani Quartet while collaborating on the Mendelssohn Octet.[1] He was inspired by his Cleveland String Quartet colleague Paul Katz. Paul's concept was to imagine creating a mood through theater lighting and then represent it through the sound. Based on this concept, Peter helped us listen strategically by inviting us to imagine we were shining a light that reflects the mood and character on the person playing the melodic line. He would then say, "Send your part, or shine the light across to support your colleague to express the character."

Ensemble members illuminate the melody through physical motion and visual contact by employing *shining the light*. The nonmelodic voices are not merely a background to the melody—you must actively inspire and support your colleagues. This technique is an exercise that develops empathy and awareness among group members. As a result, players with nonmelodic lines become actively engaged in the music-making experience.

This technique facilitates decisions regarding balance. *Shining the light* increases awareness of different musical textures, such as homophonic or polyphonic textures (see Table 10.1 in the chapter "Techniques for Intonation").

The Art of Collaboration. Annie Fullard and Dorianne Cotter-Lockard, Oxford University Press. © Oxford University Press 2025.
DOI: 10.1093/oso/9780197673126.003.0014

Techniques for Strategic Listening and Balance   163

✓ While playing, imagine using your body language to project the sound as if you are shining a light on the person playing the melody or main thematic material. Imagine passing a cup of tea or your favorite beverage around to each quartet member as they take a turn in the spotlight.
✓ Make a visual and physical connection between yourself and the person playing the melodic line.
✓ When your role functions as harmony, think of your part as enhancing and supporting the melodic line.

In the Mendelssohn Octet, a beautiful melody in the fourth violin part is enhanced when the other players *shine the light* toward that player. Everyone in the ensemble should direct their sound toward the fourth violin. This practice deepens your perception and helps maintain a soft dynamic and appropriate balance. Figure 13.1 indicates where the melody passes from the fourth to the third violin—the players with whole notes will shine the light on the players who have the melody.

FIGURE 13.1 Shining the Light, Mendelssohn Octet for Strings in E-flat Major, Op. 20, Allegro moderato con fuoco.

The Listening Game

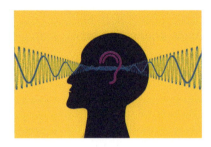

FIGURE 13.2 Sound waves. (image by Gerd Altmann from Pixabay)

The listening game is a creative way to expand listening skills and knowledge of the score. The key is active, focused listening (see Figure 13.2). Each section of players in a large ensemble can focus on an adjacent person. Alternatively, the strings can focus on the woodwinds and vice versa.

- ✓ Ensemble members focus their visual and aural attention on one person or section at a time.
- ✓ Focus on all aspects of that individual's (or section's) approach to the music. Observe how they cue, move, and apply nuance and dynamics related to their part. Do they play melody, harmony, or counterpoint?
- ✓ String players: Observe your colleague's bowing and left hand.
- ✓ Wind and brass players: Observe your colleague's breathing and embouchure.

Follow these steps to practice *The Listening Game*:

1. Listen to and watch only the person or section to your right while playing a passage.
2. Reverse the process to focus only on the person or section to your left.
3. Focus on the person or section diagonally from you (add variations based on the number of people in the ensemble).

Once integrated into your normal routine, this technique becomes second nature—you become a *strategic listener* capable of contributing more to the ensemble's performance.

Switching Seats

> With my trio, we'll do things like change seats. I'll sit where the violinist is, because with a piano trio, the proximity to the piano and which side

you sit on changes the way you hear the piano. Listening is critically important.

~ Ronald Crutcher, cellist, President Emeritus, University of Richmond

This technique empowers group members to change perspectives and experience the music differently. Switching seats uses a somatic and spatial change to stimulate a perceptual shift among ensemble members.[2] Cavani Quartet cellist, Kyle Price, appreciates the rehearsal technique of switching seats. He explains:

> It helps you hear parts differently than before. When you return to your normal seats, you have an awareness of everyone's part. You begin to realize, "Okay, my line is maybe not as important as I thought it was here. And I'm going to inspire my colleague to play theirs out." (Kyle Price)

Be flexible and approach this technique as an expansion of your expressive capabilities as individuals and as an ensemble. Here are the steps to practice this technique:

1. Move to a different position than your usual position within the ensemble.
2. Play a passage or an entire movement of a work—focus on the sound and how it has altered in this new configuration. You may want to remain in the new configuration for the rest of the rehearsal.
3. Rotate to a new seating, play the same passage, and repeat as desired.
4. Return to your original seating—discuss what you noticed.

If you do not agree on which seating arrangement works best for the ensemble, ask a friend, colleague, or coach to listen to the group with eyes closed while you try each configuration. Use your new perception of sound to catalyze deeper listening and musical exploration—you may change your usual setup for the next performance.

Playing with Backs to Each Other

This technique enables ensemble members to listen to and sense the other members without visual contact. It promotes listening acuity and synchronous breathing. This technique redefines the way you listen for balance. Playing with your backs to each other causes ensemble members to develop "extra radar," which promotes equal voicing.

1. Turn your chairs and stands around or stand and face the outside walls of the space.

166 The Art of Collaboration

2. Play a passage with your backs to each other.
3. Each person takes a turn as initiator.
4. Give a strong cue through the breath.
5. Listen for articulation, phrasing, and rhythmic alignment.
6. Become aware of how you are breathing together.

14

THE CAPSTONE TECHNIQUE

LIVE, BREATHE, AND DIE (LBAD)

> Live, Breathe and Die is one of the most important rehearsal techniques I learned from the Cavani String Quartet while I was a graduate student. LBAD was a game changer for me as a student and it continues to be a beloved pedagogical tool of mine in helping students understand how to both listen and offer up ideas. Listening with your full attention to another's intention is a profoundly difficult task, as it requires setting aside one's ego and agenda while deeply engaging in the perspective of another.
>
> ~ Elizabeth Oakes, violist, Director, University of Iowa String Quartet Program

This chapter focuses on the capstone technique of *Live, Breath, and Die (LBAD)*. This technique represents the culmination of our interpretive and expressive process. Our former and current students have all found *LBAD* to be transformational. This practice ensures that ensemble members relate to each other by initiating (cueing), reflecting, and responding.

We build this technique on the foundation of a mirroring practice used in theater, which helps students to experience initiation, reflection, and response. The mirroring technique distills the essence of *LBAD* into visual, nonverbal movement.

In This Chapter:

- Theater Mirroring Exercise
- *LBAD*

Theater Mirroring Exercise

> Chamber music is a great laboratory, and it is a great experience for collaboration and interpersonal skills that you can take into your daily life.
>
> ~ Paul Katz, former member, Cleveland String Quartet

The *Theater Mirroring Exercise* was adapted from improvisational theater games, first developed by Viola Spolin.[1] This exercise serves as a prelude to *LBAD*. We offer it to our students to experience mirroring each other's physical expressions and

The Art of Collaboration. Annie Fullard and Dorianne Cotter-Lockard, Oxford University Press. © Oxford University Press 2025. DOI: 10.1093/oso/9780197673126.003.0015

breathing without using instruments or props (see Figure 14.1). Scientific research shows that our brains have mirror neurons that reflect our emotions back to others.[2] Other research shows that when two or more people are playing music in total synchronization, our brain waves, heart rates, and other physiological systems also move together and harmonize.[3] This process is called *entrainment*.

As a precursor to *LBAD*, the *Theater Mirroring Exercise* involves the process of mirroring to improve cueing and concentration, helping create an ensemble that moves and plays together. This exercise develops nonverbal sensing abilities and awareness, and can also improve coordination and enhance creativity. Ensemble members accomplish this technique without instruments, but it requires focused attention on your partner. We now list the steps to implement the *Theater Mirroring Exercise*.

1. In dyads (two people), stand facing each other an arm's length apart.
2. Decide who will be the first *initiator* of movement and who will be the *mirror*.
3. In silence, the initiator holds one hand up with palm open, as if about to give a "high five."
4. Without touching, the mirror holds their hand up with palm open to reflect the initiator's hand position (if the initiator puts up their left hand, the mirror matches with their right hand).
5. The initiator moves their hand in a circular motion and the mirror reflects the exact motion, including the speed and pattern of motion.
6. Partners can expand the motion in creative ways that allows the mirroring to continue with ease.

Here are additional notes about this technique to take into consideration as you practice this integral exercise leading to *LBAD*. You can view an example of this technique in a video called *The Mirror Game*, created by Laughter for a Change.[4] The famous video of Harpo Marx and Lucille Ball performing a mirroring sequence can be seen on YouTube.[5]

FIGURE 14.1 *Theater Mirroring Exercise*, Weatherhead School of Business, Coaching Research Laboratory, session facilitated by Cavani Quartet. (Photo credit: Collin Arnold)

The Capstone Technique: Live, Breathe, and Die (LBAD)   **169**

✓ Both parties are responsible for a successful mirroring process.
✓ The initiator is responsible to perform movements in a way that the mirror can follow precisely.
✓ Each round usually goes for 30–60 seconds.
✓ Switch roles and repeat.

The *Theater Mirroring Exercise* serves as a prelude to coaching and rehearsal with newly formed groups, for musicians who are playing chamber music for the first time. Established ensembles will find this exercise refreshing and helpful for creating connection between members. The activity helps people to get to know each other in a nonverbal manner. While it is not necessary to perform this exercise before you try the *LBAD* technique, we find the practice is a way to generate empathetic and somatic awareness. The experience of the *Theater Mirroring Exercise* transforms how members of any group, including nonmusicians, relate to each other as a self-directed team.

LBAD

> At the beginning it's not really molded together. It's like unfired clay. As a result of LBAD, each person is influenced by what they just heard, what they liked, what they didn't like, and by their own ideas. And, by the time each person has taken a turn, it becomes collective. Finally, you play the passage with everyone initiating. I think LBAD is the kiln.
>
> ~ Alex Cox, cellist, Thalea String Quartet

The phrase *Live, Breathe, and Die* refers to a total commitment to live in the moment together, breathe through the music, and allow one's ego to "die" in service to other members' musical intentions. Music lives through the process of connecting with each other. Breathing together is an organic source of connection between human beings. When we breathe together, we share space and energy. Our colleague, French horn player and former Imani Winds member, Jeff Scott reminds us that "in chamber music, you don't just play the music, you *share* the music."

The goal of *LBAD* is to breathe with and mirror every motion and musical nuance of the initiator. The initiator, feeling supported by their colleagues, steps up to inspire them. *LBAD* requires active physical, mental, and emotional engagement from all group members. There are no "leaders" or "followers." The roles in this technique are defined as *initiators* and *responders*. These are the steps in the *LBAD* technique:

1. Each member takes a turn initiating a selected musical passage.
2. The initiator demonstrates their musical interpretation through cueing, movement, facial expression, and energy. The objective is for the initiator to *share* their musical ideas and *inspire* their colleagues.

3. All ensemble members should "be up" (have an active stance focused on the center of the group) and visual connection with the initiator at least once per measure.
4. Responders imitate *every* physical gesture and musical nuance of the initiator, as if you are the mirror reflecting back to the initiator.
5. Responders incorporate the rhythmic character, dynamics, and articulations of the initiator.
6. The initiator actively inspires and engages with ensemble members, reacting in the moment, building on the energy they receive from the group.
7. Repeat these steps until everyone in the ensemble has taken a turn as initiator.

LBAD improves group relations and allows for an openness to embrace new ideas and musical interpretations. *LBAD* helps ensembles cultivate trust through active reflection of each other's movement, breathing, and interpretation. *LBAD* offers opportunities to try something that is out of one's comfort zone and changes the way we listen. This technique also encompasses deep listening and sensing each other, and can be equally impactful with musicians who are visually impaired.

Many current and former students of the Cavani Quartet incorporate *LBAD* into their regular rehearsal process. The members of the Jupiter Quartet participated as students in the Intensive Quartet Seminar taught by the Cavani String Quartet and Peter Salaff. Meg Freivogel, violinist of the Jupiter Quartet tells the following story about *LBAD*.

> In the Jupiter Quartet, our favorite rehearsal technique is "Live, Breathe, and Die" (*LBAD* for short). Yes, a bit of a dramatic name but you never forget it! In this technique, you learn to follow, imitate, and mirror one person in the group while playing your own part. This is meant for working out a small section, taking turns leading and following. It informs us about the nuances of how someone is feeling about a particular section. We learn to support an idea without getting in the way and also how to make it even more beautiful and complex. I often think that if we employed this approach to all collaborations, it would empower and inspire more people while avoiding frustration and conflict. But chamber music is a perfect place to start! (Meg Freivogel)

Dorianne's research with students of the Cavani Quartet showed that ensemble members felt fully supported by their colleagues during live performances as a result of practicing *LBAD* during rehearsals. They reported that they no longer felt alone when playing certain passages, and that *LBAD* helped them to embody a combined interpretation and presentation of the music. This process alleviated performance anxiety and empowered students to raise the level of their performances to greater heights of excellence.[6]

The Cavani Quartet finds that the *LBAD* process creates a living thread of communication that enables greater technical facility and freedom, and increases the spontaneous quality of music-making. This is the dream that every teacher hopes

The Capstone Technique: Live, Breathe, and Die (LBAD) **171**

for, where students take an idea or practice and make it their own. Annie recently heard a transcendent performance of the complete *Goldberg Variations* by J. S. Bach, arranged for quartet by the members of the Catalyst Quartet. Their intertwined and conversational approach was stunning—she witnessed four individuals as one powerful voice. The Catalyst Quartet often speaks about their use of *LBAD* in rehearsal and as a teaching tool. In their soaring performance of the *Goldberg Variations*, the impact of *LBAD* was fully evident. We are humbled and grateful to witness so many professional string quartets and conductorless ensembles which use *LBAD* in their rehearsals.

APPENDIX A

Resources

This list of resources that we turn to frequently for reference is provided as an addition to those listed in the bibliography. It is organized by topic and is not intended be exhaustive.

- General Chamber Music Resources
- Music Resources—History and Theory
- Chamber Music Rehearsal Techniques
- Chamber Music Pedagogy
- Chamber Music Biographies
- Learning and Practicing Music
- Music Glossaries and Dictionaries
- Resources for Scores
- Collaboration and Leadership
- Mind-Body Resources for Musicians
- Website Related to Chamber Music

General Chamber Music Resources

Berger, M. (2013). *Guide to chamber music*. Dover Publications.

Brentano Quartet. (2023). *Program notes*. https://www.brentanoquartet.com/notes/

Dogantan-Dack, M. (2022). *The chamber musician in the twenty-first century*. MDPI-Multidisciplinary Digital Publishing Institute.

Fink, I., Merriell, C., & Guarneri String Quartet. (1985). *String quartet playing*. Paganiniana Publications.

Jeffery, P. (2017). *A player's guide to chamber music*. The Crowood Press.

Keller, J. (2010). *Chamber music: A listener's guide*. Oxford University Press.

Monsman, N. (2018). *A friend's guide to chamber music: European trends from Haydn to Shostakovich*. Cathedral Rock Art.

Timmers, R., Bailes, F., & Daffern, H. (Eds.). (2021). *Together in music: Coordination, expression, participation*. Oxford University Press.

Music Resources—History and Theory

Antokoletz, E. (1984). *The music of Béla Bartók: A study of tonality and progression in twentieth-century music*. University of California Press.

Bandy, D. K. (2023). *Mozart the performer: Variations on the showman's art*. University of Chicago Press.

Beer, A. (2016). *Sounds and sweet airs: The forgotten women of classical music*. Simon and Schuster.

Beethoven, L. van (2011). *Beethoven's Letters 1790–1826* (Vol. 1) (G. Wallace, Trans.; first published 1866, Oliver Ditson & Co.). Public Domain Book digitized by volunteers.

Berry, W. (1985). *Form in music* (2nd ed.). Pearson.

Berry, W. (1987). *Structural functions in music*. Courier Corporation.

Brault, Olivier: Canadian violinist and member of The Four Nations Ensemble and Apollo's Fire, specializes in the Baroque and Classical repertoire. https://www.fournations.org/olivier-brault and https://apollosfire.org/dvteam/olivier-brault/

Dusinberre, E. (2017). *Beethoven for a later age: Living with the string quartets*. University of Chicago Press.

Hutchinson, E. O. (2016). *It's our music too: The black experience in classical music*. Middle Passage Press.

Isacoff, S. (2011). *A natural history of the piano: The instrument, the music, the musicians—From Mozart to modern jazz, and everything in between*. Knopf.

174   Appendix A: Resources

Klorman, E. (2016). *Mozart's music of friends: Social interplay in the chamber works*. Cambridge University Press.

Lockwood, L. (2008). *Inside Beethoven's quartets: History, performance, interpretation*. Harvard University Press.

Mirka, D. (2021). *Hypermetric manipulations in Haydn and Mozart: Chamber music for strings, 1787–1791*. Oxford University Press.

Rosen, C. (1988). *Sonata forms*. WW Norton & Company.

Rosen, C. (1998). *The classical style: Haydn, Mozart, Beethoven*. WW Norton & Company.

Schoenberg, A. (1999). *Structural functions of harmony*. Faber & Faber Academic.

Sumner Lott, M. (2015). *The social worlds of nineteenth-century chamber music: Composers, consumers, communities*. University of Illinois Press.

Swafford, J. (2012). *Johannes Brahms: A biography*. Vintage.

Swafford, J. (2014). *Beethoven: Anguish and triumph*. Faber & Faber.

Swafford, J. (2020). *Mozart: The reign of love*. Faber & Faber.

Tomes, S. (2021). *The piano: A history in 100 pieces*. Yale University Press.

Chamber Music Rehearsal Techniques

Dunhill, T. F. (1913). *Chamber music: A treatise for students*. Macmillan.

Heimann, M. (2007). *Exercises for string quartet* (M. Deckert, Ed.). ACMP, ESTA.

Hochmiller, S. (2018). *So you want to sing chamber music: A guide for performers*. Rowman & Littlefield.

Léner, J. (1935). *The technique of string quartet playing*. Chester.

Loft, A. P. R. G. (1992). *Ensemble! A rehearsal guide to thirty great works of chamber music*. Amadeus Press.

Norton, M. D. H. (1925). *The art of string quartet playing: Practice, technique, and interpretation*. Simon and Schuster.

Page, A. (1964). *Playing string quartets*. Longmans.

Stéphan, F. (English version Schell, E., 2009). *String quartet self-coaching*. ACMP.

Padilla, G. (2021). *Chamber music fundamentals and rehearsal techniques for advancing string students* [Doctoral Dissertation, West Virginia University].

Chamber Music Pedagogy

Balcom, D., & Porter Tall, S. (2014). *Building a chamber music program: A teacher's guide*. Chamber Music Society of Lincoln Center. https://www.academia.edu/23709041/Chamber_musiC_Program_A_TeAchers_Guide

International Suzuki Association contains instructional videos and resources for learning stringed instruments. https://internationalsuzuki.org/

Music Teachers National Association has a section of parent and student resources with links to educational websites, mostly for children. https://www.mtna.org/

National Association for Music Education has resources and lessons sections. https://nafme.org/

The American Viola Society: https://www.americanviolasociety.org/

Chamber Music Biographies

Blum, D., & Guarneri String Quartet. (1986). *The art of quartet playing: The Guarneri Quartet in conversation with David Blum*. Knopf.

Blum, D. (1999). *Quintet: Five journeys toward musical fulfillment*. Cornell University Press.

Brown, R. L. (2020). *The heart of a woman: The life and music of Florence B. Price*. University of Illinois Press.

Loft, A. (2003). *How to succeed in an ensemble: Reflections on a life in chamber music*. Amadeus Press.

Mann, R. (2018). *A passionate journey: A memoir*. East End Press.

Rounds, D., & Lafayette String Quartet. (1999). *The four and the one: In praise of string quartets*. Lost Coast Press.

Simmenauer, S. (2023). *Two violins, a viola, a cello and me*. (G. O. Robinson & H. Kuhlmann Trans.). Harcamlow Press. (Original work published 2008, 2nd edition, 2021)

Snowman, D. (1981). *The Amadeus Quartet: The men and the music*. Robson Books.

Tomes, S. (2004). *Beyond the notes: Journeys with chamber music*. Boydell Press.

Learning and Practicing Music

Bruser, M. (1997). *The art of practicing: A guide to making music from the heart*. Three Rivers Press.

Flesch, C., & (2008). *The art of violin playing: Book 1* (E. Rosenblith, Ed.). Carl Fischer.

Galamian, I., & Neumann, F. (1966). *Contemporary violin technique*. Galaxy Music Corporation.

International Society for Music Education: https://www.isme.org/

Laws, C. (Ed.). (2020). *Performance, subjectivity, and experimentation*. Leuven University Press.

Menuhin, Y. (1971). *Violin: Six lessons with Yehudi Menuhin*. The Viking Press.

Steinhardt, A. (2013). *The teaching wisdom of violinist Joseph Szigeti*. The Strad. https://www.thestrad.com/the-teaching-wisdom-of-violinist-joseph-szigeti/5550.article#commentsJump

Williamon, A. (Ed.). (2004). *Musical excellence: Strategies and techniques to enhance performance*. Oxford University Press.

Music Dictionaries and Glossaries

Los Angeles Chamber Orchestra glossary of musical terms: https://www.laco.org/visit/glossary/

Oxford and Grove Music Online: https://www.oxfordmusiconline.com/grovemusic

ONMusic Dictionary: https://dictionary.onmusic.org/

NAXOS Glossary of musical terms: https://www.naxos.com/Glossary/ABC

Yale University Library, Glossary of musical forms: https://web.library.yale.edu/cataloging/music/Basic-glossary-of-musical-terms

Resources for Scores

International Music Score Library Project (IMSLP)-Petrucci Music Library is an online resource for public domain music parts and scores. https://imslp.org/wiki/Main_Page.

Music by Black Composers is a reference source related to composers of color. https://www.musicbyblackcomposers.org/; Living Black Composers Directory: https://www.musicbyblackcomposers.org/resources/living-composers-directory/; Historic Black Composers Directory: https://www.musicbyblackcomposers.org/resources/historic-composers-directory/

New Music Box/Native American Composers: https://newmusicusa.org/nmbx/native-american-composers/

Commercial sources for scores and parts include SHAR, Sheet Music Plus, SilverTrust, Amazon, Dover Publications, Barenreiter, Boosey & Hawkes, and Henle.

Collaboration and Leadership

Boyatzis, R. E., & McKee, A. (2005). *Resonant leadership: Renewing yourself and connecting with others through mindfulness, hope, and compassion*. Harvard Business Press.

Brown, B. (2018). *Dare to lead: Brave work. Tough conversations. Whole Hearts*. Random House.

David L. Cooperrider Center for Appreciative Inquiry at Champlain College, & Case Western University, Weatherhead School of Management. (n.d.). *Appreciative inquiry commons*. https://appreciativeinquiry.champlain.edu/

176   Appendix A: Resources

Hougaard, R., & Carter, J. (2022). *Compassionate leadership: How to do hard things in a human way.* HBR Press.

Ippolito, L. M. (2019). *Music, leadership, and conflict: The art of ensemble negotiation and problem-solving.* Springer.

Kerrigan, S. (2016). *The performer's guide to the collaborative process.* Lulu Press, Inc.

Lerman, L. & Borstel, J. (2022). *Critique is creative: The Critical Response Process® in theory and action.* Wesleyan University Press.

McKee, A., Boyatzis, R. E., & Johnston, F. (2008). *Becoming a resonant leader: Develop your emotional intelligence, renew your relationships, sustain your effectiveness.* Harvard Business Press.

Nankivell, B. (2015, December 24). *Emotional intelligence by Daniel Goleman—Animated book summary.* [Video]. YouTube. https://youtu.be/n6MRsGwyMuQ

Olafsson, T., Allenby, S., & Tuck, K. (2022). *Beyond ego—The inner compass of conscious leadership.* New Leadership Press.

Sawyer, K. (2014). Group creativity: Musical performance and collaboration. In R. Caines & A. Heble (Eds.), *The improvisation studies reader* (pp. 87–100). Routledge.

Sawyer, K. (2017). *Group genius: The creative power of collaboration.* Basic Books.

Schein, E., & Schein, P. (2018). *Humble leadership: The power of relationships, openness, and trust.* Berrett-Koehler.

Sinek, S. (2017, August 2). *Understanding empathy.* [Video]. YouTube. https://youtu.be/pi86Nr9Mdms

The Ensemble Project explores the relationship between music and empathy. https://www.theensemble project.com/

Mind-Body Resources for Musicians

Alexander Technique for Musicians: https://alexandertechnique.com/musicians/

BAPNE Method (*Biomecánica. Anatomía. Psicología. Neurociencia. Etnomusicología*: Biomechanics, Anatomy, Psychology, Neuroscience, Ethnomusicology): https://percusion-corporal.com

Carlson, L. H. (2021). *How mindfulness helps musicians perform—Research and techniques.* Mindful Leader. https://www.mindfulleader.org/blog/58707-how-mindfulness-helps-musicians

Cornett, V. (2019). *The mindful musician: Mental skills for peak performance.* Oxford University Press. Companion website with resources: https://global.oup.com/us/companion.websites/9780190864613/

Dalcroze eurhythmics is a process for awakening, developing, and refining innate musicality through rhythmic movement, ear training, and improvisation. https://dalcrozeusa.org

Kleinman, J., & Buckoke, P. (2013). *The Alexander technique for musicians.* A&C Black.

Levitan, D. (2006). *This is your brain on music.* A Plume Book.

Mindfulness for Musicians. Center for Mindfulness, The Netherlands. https://centrumvoormindfuln ess.nl/en/mindfulness-for-musicians/

Your Body Is Your Strad (YBIYS) Institute, Feldenkrais for Musicians focuses on the importance of awareness to understand functions of the real instrument—your body and mind—to help maximize musical communication and minimize injury in performance through the Feldenkrais Method. http://www.harmoniousmovement.com/

Website Resources Related to Chamber Music

ACMP (The Chamber Music Network) has brief documents and videos to guide amateur musicians in learning chamber music. https://acmp.net/

Banff International String Quartet Festival: https://www.banffcentre.ca/banff-international-string-quartet-festival

Chamber Music America: https://chambermusicamerica.org/

Chamber Music International: http://www.chambermusicinternational.org/

Earsense contains a database of chamber-music compositions. Each composition has a page associated with it, and each page contains biographical information about the composer, notes about the composition, and either audio or video recordings. https://www.earsense.org/

Eastman School of Music Sibley Library Resources: https://www.esm.rochester.edu/sibley/resources/

Fischoff Chamber Music Competition: https://www.fischoff.org/

Seiji Ozawa International Academy: https://ozawa-academy.ch/en/academy/

APPENDIX B

Descriptive Words

This list of descriptive words was originally created by the students at The Encore String Quartet Intensive and compiled by Joseph Kromholz (violinist, faculty Luther College) and Cavani String Quartet members. Further edits were made to the content of this appendix—it serves as an example of choices to inspire your interpretive conversation. Use this list when you need a little extra help during rehearsals to describe a musical character or mood.

Happiness		
Joy	Peaceful	Heroic
Jovial	Tranquil	Gallant
Exuberance	Dreamy	Grandiose
Elation	Easygoing	Pompous
Delight	Placid	Prancing
Jouissance	Lull	Courageous
Fierce	Breezy	Brave
Ecstatic	Lush	Fearless
Euphoric	Warm	Acrobatic
Giddy	Rich	Dancing
Vigor	Excitement	Effervescent
Invigorating	Anticipation	Ebullient
Dramatic	Hopeful	Piquant
Energetic	Eager	Lyrical
Rejuvenated	Thrill	Buoyant
Blissful	Exhilarated	Bouncing
Bemused	Earnest	Wonderous
Satisfied	Expectant	Wonderment
Contentment	Triumphant	Carefree
Serene	Grand	
Affection		
Wistful	Teasing	Reverent
Intoxicated	Coy	Trusting
Besotted	Tender	Heart-warming
Obsessive	Dreamy	Acceptance
Sensuous	Charming	Innig/Intimate (German)
Sultry	Admiringly	Childlike
Flirtatious	Devoted	Impassioned
		Vulnerable
Humor		
Scherzando	Witty	Wry
Fun	Teasing	Winking
Laughing	Playful	Sardonic
Joking	Lighthearted	Tongue-in-cheek
Cheeky	Flirtatious	Wily

180 Appendix B: Descriptive Words

Anger

Brooding	Forceful	Obsessive
Vehement	Stiff	Implacable
Fierce	Clamorous	Sarcastic
Raging	Strident	Caustic
Fuming	Furious	Brutal
Seething	Wrath	Menacing
Igniting	Resentful	Imposing
Fiery	Agitated	Indifference
Reluctant	Frustrated	Cold
Irascible	Obstinate	Icy
Huffy	Stubborn	Crying
Complaining	Relentless	Sobbing

Fear

Foreboding	Ghostly	Inquiring
Uncertain	Careful	Angst
Shy	Anxious	Dread
Lost	Apprehensive	Tremulous
Adrift	Frenzied	Frozen
Wandering	Pleading	Timorous
Searching	Beseeching	Terrified
Nervous	Gasping	Questioning
Suspicious	Heaving	Wondering
Timid	Breathless	Begging
Probing	Courageous (see *Happiness*)	

Sadness

Mourning	Hollow	Despair
Brooding	Numb	Sorrow
Nostalgic	Gloomy	Wilting
Grief-stricken	Morose	Plaintive
Sorrowful	Lugubrious	Longing (see *Affection*)
Lonely	Despondent	Resignation
Hopeless	Stagnant	Acceptance
Depressed	Heartbroken	Wistful
Drained	Tragic	Frustration (see *Anger*)
Exhausted	Cathartic	Disappointed
Dejected	Wailing	Melancholy
Bleak	Anguished	Lonely
Empty		

Surprise

Awe	Mystery	Startled
Amazed	Mysterious	Uncertainty
Astonished	Shocking	Wonder
Astounded	Startling	Unresolved
Wonder		

Appendix B: Descriptive Words

Other		
Fleeting	Clumsy	Din
Passing	Lumbering	Racket
Solemn	Oozing	Remote
Noble	Snappy	Thoughtful
Regal	Spicy	Pensive
Stately	Unbalanced	Extroverted
Elegant	Crooked	Introverted
Poised	Lopsided	Stoic
Courteous	Determined	Immovable
Courtly	Steely	Impassive
Galant	Gritty	Vacillating
Gracious	Innocent	Undulating
Delicate	Spiritual	Suppressed
Fragile	Divine	Certain
Tiptoeing	Ethereal	Uncertain
Inward	Awe	Wondering
Limping	Chaos	Sunny
Skipping	Ruckus	Conversational
Leaping	Piercing	Intertwined

APPENDIX C

Rehearsal Plan Summary

Chamber music playing empowers you to develop artistic freedom, expression, and empathy. Each ensemble member should function as part of a collaborative team and share equal leadership responsibility. Use this guide as a starting point for individual preparation and applying key points from this book to your rehearsal process.

Organize Your Part and Score

✓ **Every ensemble member should have their own score.**
Suggested editions: Barenreiter, Henle, or Peters. Other editions are also useful sources for articulation. Remember that Barenreiter and Henle editions are also edited—be proactively involved in the interpretive process based on informed musical and contextual knowledge. In other words, do not choose to follow a marking only because it is "there." We encourage experimentation.
✓ **Keep your part and score in a binder, or use a tablet or other electronic device.**
✓ **Bring a pencil or stylus and a tuner or tuner app to rehearsal.**
✓ **Write measure numbers in your part and score if they are not already included.**

Learn Your Part Carefully

Learning your part before rehearsal is the first priority of ensemble playing and enables a great chamber music experience. Even if your part looks simple, the experience of playing it with others for the first time will be different. Therefore, the better you know your part, the easier it will be to play together.

✓ **Practice slowly** (see Itzhak Perlman's "Itzhak on Practicing" on YouTube).
✓ **Dynamics:** Observe the dynamics carefully. Circle extremes, such as *crescendo* starts at the softest volume level and *diminuendo* begins at the loudest or climactic moment of the musical phrase.
✓ **Rhythm:** Practice with precise rhythm, cueing yourself in after rests. Count difficult rhythms and all rests out loud.
✓ **Use the metronome** as a practice partner to help you feel a consistent rhythmic pulse.
✓ **Chamber music playing** is about musical conversation within and across an ensemble. Practice looking up and out of your part as if you are passing your line to another ensemble member.

Use Media as Resource

✓ **Listen to other works by the composer** (e.g., symphonies, ballet, opera, art songs, etc.).
✓ **Listen to a variety of recordings by different artists:** Note aspects that you enjoy related to the sound, tempo, character, and ensemble.
✓ **Avoid copying interpretations:** Use recordings to understand how your part fits with the others and make interpretive decisions as a group.
✓ **Listen with eyes closed or in a relaxed way:** Fall in love with your piece.

Score Study

✓ **Listen with the score:** As you explore, analyze, and interpret the score, you will appreciate the composer's intent and gain a thorough knowledge of all the parts of the ensemble. Listening with the score improves your ability to respond to and fit in with the other parts.
✓ **Listen with your part and write in cues.**

184 Appendix C: Rehearsal Plan Summary

Be Curious

✓ **Research** the era of the composition and learn about the social, political, cultural, and artistic context, and the composer's life story.
✓ **Research** all words in the score that you do not understand.
✓ **Share Information:** Bring a fun fact to your first coaching session or rehearsal.

The Rehearsal Flow: 1 Hour

5 minutes Tune carefully, individually, and then as a group, using a tuner.
5 minutes Warm up with scales, a Bach Chorale, or a chorale of your choice.
5–10 minutes Play through movement.
Make an active effort to communicate with each other while you play—look up, cue, respond, and reflect.
20–30 minutes Spots: Each member takes a turn (5–10 minutes) to rehearse spots.

Begin by discussing character or mood, based on what you know about composer. You may then choose to focus on different details such as harmonic motion, intonation, dynamics, or rhythmic alignment.

Problem solving: match articulation, exaggerate dynamics, take turns cuing beginning or end of phrase, highlight voices with the motive or melody, check tempos, play a passage through slowly, or use the *Live, Breathe, and Die* (*LBAD*) technique.

Try every idea as if it is your own and encourage experimentation.

You can use a timer to ensure equal participation by each member.

Write ideas in your part once agreed upon.

10 minutes Play through piece or section again with goals in mind.

Rules of Collaboration and Secrets to Success

✓ Be a kind and generous colleague: make general rather than personal statements
✓ Try every idea as if it were your own
✓ Use the rule of agreement: "Yes, and . . ."
✓ Move together, breathe together
✓ Be conversational: Make it a goal to look up and make a visual connection with another group member once per bar.
✓ Humor and silliness are welcome!

APPENDIX D

Sound Production Techniques
for Strings: The Bow

Appendix D includes detailed guidance from Annie Fullard for organizing bowings and approaching bow technique related to interpretation and the rehearsal process, as introduced in the chapter "Techniques for Sound Production."

Organizing Bowing in Rehearsal

Unifying bow technique and organizing the bowings are integral for group sound production and interpretation. While bowing choices may be subjective, they should be made relative to the phrasing, articulation, and dynamics. Tempo and style considerations also influence bowing. Consider the musical markings and the composer's intent to determine the sound quality and character of the passage. Numerous combinations of bow speed, pressure, bow angle, and contact point can be generated to create a variety of colors and characters. This process of discovery should be creative and joyful.

Most string ensembles prefer to match bowing and articulation to create a feeling of alignment and highlight structural elements in the score. However, different, unmatched bowings can be used to create a variety of texture and color within a musical passage. Experimentation is vital, so try all ideas until you find something that expresses your musical point of view and works for the ensemble. The following guidelines provide rehearsal techniques for bowing solutions related to sound production:

✓ Begin by matching bowings to create a synchronized feeling among the group. Recognize that exceptions to this approach will depend on the musical context.
✓ In general, begin louder dynamics or downbeats with a down-bow.
✓ Consider beginning soft dynamics (e.g., *p*, *pp*) or pick-ups to a phrase or measure with an up-bow. A good example of starting with an up-bow is the opening measure of the Ravel String Quartet. In softer dynamics, you can also experiment with a pick-up on a down-bow at the very tip.
✓ Always breathe yourself in before beginning a passage to achieve vocal quality and release tension in the body.
✓ Play passages together, focusing only on matching the same part of the bow, with similar sound quality, dynamics, pressure, bow speed, and length.
✓ Experiment! Play the same passage together as an ensemble at the frog, in the middle, in the upper half, and at the tip. Discuss which part of the bow achieves your musical goal and produces the most cohesive group sound. Perhaps a combination of all three sections of the bow will work best!
✓ Demonstrate bowings for each other.
✓ Demonstrate bowings while other members listen with their eyes closed.
✓ Write your bowing decisions into your parts.
✓ Consider playing a repeated phrase with a different bowing the second time to create variety and express greater or less emphasis depending on the musical shape and dynamic landscape.

Bow markings may be adjusted from rehearsal to rehearsal and performance to performance due to acoustics and interpretive choices. It can be helpful for one or two ensemble members to take turns listening from outside the group to determine which bowings work best to articulate the sound and character for that passage.

186 Appendix D: Sound Production Techniques for Strings: The Bow

Techniques to Practice Bow Use

The following section begins with guidelines for playing open strings related to a musical passage. You will find guidance on the combinations of four aspects of bow technique that help determine interpretation and sound production.

Open Strings Alone

Playing a passage only with open strings alleviates concern about left-hand technique and maintains the focus on choreographing a musical passage through sound production. The following steps will guide your process for achieving a more beautiful and nuanced sound.

1. Imagine the vocal quality you seek for a passage. Consider the timbre (overtones and resonance) and core of the sound you wish to achieve. For example, is it a light and airy sounding "OO" or deep intense "AH" or bright and vibrant "EE?" Sing the sound before you play.
2. Decide if the sound should begin with a consonant (direct, for example, *marcato*) or vowel sound (*legato*).
3. Play the passage using only open strings, following all the bowings, articulations, and dynamics.
4. Play all notes as written—notice how your sound quality improves through bow awareness.

Bow Speed

An awareness of bow speed at the beginning and ending of strokes is essential to good ensemble playing. Faster bow speed produces more overtones, adding resonance. Slow bow speed can be effective in quieter passages. Bow speed combined with pressure produces a variety of tonal colors, from transparent to opaque. Focus on matching bow speed in your group warmup routine and scales.

Bow Pressure

Pressure on the bow is produced by using the first and second fingers and the thumb of the right hand in combination with the forearm. An awareness of your back and upper body posture also makes a difference in how you produce a powerful sound as a string player. Explore the full range of possible sounds. Begin by pressing down as hard as possible, which will produce a scratchy sound. Gradually reduce the amount of pressure to find the quality of sound you wish to express. Bow pressure plus speed influences the volume of sound. Combine a variety of bow speeds and pressure to achieve the sound you feel best expresses the character or mood portrayed in a musical passage.

Contact Point (Sounding Point)

The *contact* or *sounding point* is the placement of the bow in relation to the fingerboard and the bridge. Shinichi Suzuki called the point where the instrument responds most readily and most resonantly the "Kreisler highway" after famous violinist Fritz Kreisler. Renowned violin teacher Dorothy DeLay and later Simon Fischer spoke of five contact points from the bridge to the fingerboard, like five lanes on Suzuki's Kreisler highway. Each of the five lanes or contact points produces a different sound quality.[1,2]

Imagine five lanes, starting with one over the fingerboard. Practice playing a passage using each of the five lanes in succession, moving from the fingerboard to the bridge. Notice the variety in sound quality produced by playing at different contact points. Choose to vary and experiment with the contact point that best expresses the musical character.

Angle of the Bow Hair in Relation to the String

The bow hair connects to the string to create friction. As you pronate the bow stick, observe the amount of bow hair on the string. Flat bow hair produces a deep sound with greater core, while less hair in contact with the string produces a more transparent sound. As you play, experiment with a variety of bow angles.

Combine Four Aspects of Bow Technique

Combine the four aspects of bow technique (speed, pressure, contact point, and angle of hair through rotation of the stick) to deepen your interpretative process. The following are suggestions for combinations of bow techniques to express different moods or characters.

✓ For a soft, *dolce* sound, place the bow over the fingerboard, use minimal pressure and slow-to-medium bow speed, and maintain the bow angle to achieve flat hair, which produces a glowing effect.
✓ For a triumphant, joyful chord, use the entire bow, with a fast bow speed, medium pressure, and a contact point close to the bridge.
✓ For a ghostly, whispered sound, keep the bow moving and close to the fingerboard, with a thin edge of bow hair, as if you are *floating* the bow or barely hovering over the string.
✓ For a powerful, rich, and heart-wrenching sound, keep the bow moving, with flat hair, very close to the bridge, varying pressure through the note to sound deep and expressive rather than harsh or brash.
✓ In a passage that moves from soft to loud, focus on combining bow techniques, adjusting them to suit the character and color of the music. Begin in *pianissimo* at the tip of the bow, over the fingerboard, with minimal hair on the string and slow bow speed. Gradually move the contact point toward the bridge, add speed, and flatten the bow hair to produce a bright and beautiful *forte* sound.
✓ Always sense your bow hold, observe how your fingertips relate to the frog and how your hand shape adjusts as you travel between the frog and tip.

Legato Bowings

For string ensembles, producing a beautiful *legato* sound involves matching the right- and left-hand technique. Experiment with slur lengths to ensure you can vividly express moments of arrival in the music, especially when there are extreme dynamic indications.

Try the original slurred bowing first, and then adapt the bowing to one that best achieves your interpretive intent and matches the tempo and flow of the music. Bowing among ensemble members should match to unify the sound. Be open to more than one solution and enjoy the process of discovering a variety of options.

Emphasis Markings: Sforzando and Staccato

Emphasis markings such as staccato (dots or carets) accents, *tenuto*, or *sforzandos* give the music a heightened expressivity, shape, and nuance. Emphasis markings should be interpreted in the context of the dynamics surrounding them. For instance, a softer dynamic implies a gentler articulation for an accent or *sforzando*, which may grow in intensity and force. As a general approach, try *sforzando* when observed in soft dynamics at the tip, with a combination of bow speed and pressure to produce an articulation that grabs the attention without sounding harsh or aggressive. In *forte or fortissimo* dynamics, a *sforzando* can be played with considerable right- and left-hand intensity, usually in the lower half of the bow. A louder *sforzando* also demands stronger physical motion to portray the emotional and powerful nature of the music.

188 Appendix D: Sound Production Techniques for Strings: The Bow

For *staccato* and *sforzando* articulations consider the following:

✓ Match your articulation by playing in the same part of the bow.
✓ Experiment by playing *staccato* or *sforzando* articulations at different parts of the bow, such as the frog, middle, and the tip.

These suggestions are a starting point for the process of interpretation through right-hand technique and sound production.

APPENDIX E

Contributors to the Book

Appendix E contains an alphabetical list of the musicians we interviewed or had conversations with related to the book's content. We are grateful to everyone who contributed! We include links to their websites for further information.

Mike Block: cellist, Silk Road Ensemble (https://www.silkroad.org/)

Earl Carlyss: violinist, former member Juilliard String Quartet, faculty at Juilliard (https://www.juilliard.edu/music/faculty/carlyss-earl)

Charles Castleman: violinist, Director of the Castleman Quartet Program (https://www.castlemanquartetprogram.com/)

Heidi Castleman: violist, faculty at Juilliard (https://www.juilliard.edu/music/faculty/castleman-heidi)

Catherine Cosbey: violinist, member Cavani Quartet (https://cavanistringquartet.com/)

Alex Cox: cellist, Thalea Quartet (https://www.thaleastringquartet.com/)

Ronald Crutcher: cellist, President Emeritus, University of Richmond (https://music.richmond.edu/faculty/rcrutche/) and Wheaton College, member Klemperer Trio

Kirsten Docter: violist, former member Cavani Quartet, faculty Oberlin College and Conservatory of Music (https://www.oberlin.edu/kirsten-docter)

James Dunham: violist, former member Cleveland String Quartet, faculty at the Shepherd School of Music, Rice University (https://music.rice.edu/faculty/james-dunham)

Monica Ellis: bassoonist and founding member of Imani Winds (https://imaniwinds.com/)

David Finckel: former cellist Emerson Quartet and Artistic Director, Chamber Music Society of Lincoln Center (https://davidfinckelandwuhan.com/ and https://www.chambermusicsociety.org/about-us/people/artists/strings/david-finckel/)

Norman Fischer: former cellist, Concord String Quartet, faculty at the Shepherd School of Music, Rice University (https://music.rice.edu/faculty/norman-fischer)

Gabriela Lena Frank: composer, Director, Gabriela Lena Frank Creative Academy of Music (https://www.glfcam.com/).

Elizabeth Hankins: Orchestra Director, Lakewood City Schools (https://lhs.lakewoodcityschools.org/)

Paul Katz: cellist, former member Cleveland String Quartet, faculty at New England Conservatory of Music (https://necmusic.edu/faculty/paul-katz), founder CelloBello (https://www.cellobello.org/)

Martha Strongin Katz: violist, former member Cleveland String Quartet, faculty emeritus at New England Conservatory of Music (https://en.wikipedia.org/wiki/Martha_Strongin_Katz)

Ayane Kozasa: violist, Kronos Quartet, former member Aizuri Quartet, guest violist, Cavani Quartet (http://ayanekozasa.com/ and https://kronosquartet.org/)

Joel Krosnick: cellist, former member Juilliard String Quartet, chair Cello Department at Juilliard (https://www.juilliard.edu/music/faculty/krosnick-joel)

Joseph Kromholz: violinist, faculty Luther College, Iowa (https://josephkromholz.com/ and https://www.luther.edu/faculty/joseph-kromholz)

Robert Mann (deceased): founding member, former first violinist, Juilliard String Quartet (https://robertmannviolinist.com/index.html and video clip from *Speak the Music*—a documentary film by Allen Miller https://youtu.be/ZCYAd6oQrQw)

Megan Frievogel McDonough: violinist, Jupiter Quartet (https://www.jupiterquartet.com/)

Anton Nel: pianist, Head of the Division of Keyboard Studies, Butler School of Music, University of Texas at Austin (https://www.antonnel.com/ and https://music.utexas.edu/about/people/anton-nel)

Elizabeth Oakes: violist and Director, University of Iowa String Quartet Program, former member of Maia Quartet (https://music.uiowa.edu/people/elizabeth-oakes)

Peter Oundjian: former first violinist, Tokyo Quartet, former conductor Toronto Symphony and Royal Scottish National Orchestra, faculty Yale University School of Music (https://peteroundjian.com/ and https://music.yale.edu/people/peter-oundjian)

190 Appendix E: Contributors to the Book

Merry Peckham: cellist, former member Cavani Quartet, Assistant Dean and Director of Chamber Music, The Juilliard School, Director Perlman Chamber Music Programs (https://www.juilliard.edu/news/162956/merry-peckham-lead-chamber-music-juilliard and https://www.perlmannusicprogram.org/merry-peckham)

Karla Donehew Perez: violinist, Catalyst Quartet (https://catalystquartet.com/)

Deborah Price: violist and Director, Chamber Music Connection (https://cmconnection.org/ and https://iclassical-academy.com/teachers-general/deborah-pirce-viola/)

Kyle Price: cellist, member Cavani Quartet (https://kylebarrettprice.com/ and https://cavanistringquartet.com/)

Donald Rosenberg: former music critic, *Cleveland Plain Dealer* and author, *The Cleveland Orchestra Story*

Tom Rosenberg: cellist, Artistic Director, Fischoff National Chamber Music Competition, former member Chester Quartet (https://www.tomrosenbergmusic.com/Opus_1911_Music_Studio/Welcome.html and https://www.fischoff.org/)

Samuel Rosenthal: violist, Kronberg Academy (https://samuelrosenthalviola.com/)

Peter Salaff: violinist, former member Cleveland String Quartet

Mari Sato: violinist, former member Cavani Quartet (https://www.citymusiccleveland.org/mari-sato)

Amy Schwartz-Moretti: violinist, Director, Mercer University, Robert McDuffie Center for Strings (https://music.mercer.edu/faculty-and-staff/amy-moretti/)

Astrid Schween: cellist, Juilliard Quartet (https://www.astridschween.com/ and https://www.juilliardstringquartet.org/)

Jeff Scott: French horn player, founding member and former hornist of Imani Winds, faculty State University of New York at Buffalo (https://www.musicbyjeffreyscott.com/)

Vivian Hornik Weilerstein: pianist, Director Professional Piano Trio Program, piano and collaborative piano faculty, New England Conservatory of Music (https://necmusic.edu/faculty/vivian-hornik-weilerstein)

Donald Weilerstein: violinist, former member Cleveland String Quartet, faculty at New England Conservatory of Music (https://necmusic.edu/faculty/donald-weilerstein)

Carol Wincenc: flautist, former member of New York Woodwind Quintet, faculty at Juilliard (https://www.carolwincencflute.com/ and https://www.juilliard.edu/music/faculty/wincenc-carol)

Eric Wong: violist, former member Cavani Quartet, faculty Blair School of Music, Vanderbilt University (https://blair.vanderbilt.edu/bio/?pid=eric-wong)

Andrew Yee: cellist, Attacca Quartet (https://www.andrewyeecellist.com/ and http://www.attaccaquartet.com/)

Hyeyung Sol Yoon: violinist, former member Chiara Quartet, current member Del Sol Quartet (https://www.hyeyung.com/ and https://www.delsolquartet.com/)

Notes

INTRODUCTION

1. Cotter-Lockard, D. (2012). *Chamber music coaching strategies and rehearsal techniques that enable collaboration* [Doctoral Dissertation, Fielding Graduate University].
2. Kokotsaki, D., & Hallam, S. (2007). Higher education music students' perceptions of the benefits of participative music making. *Music Education Research, 9*(1), 93–109. Larson, D. D. (2010). *The effects of chamber music experience on music performance achievement, motivation, and attitudes among high school band students* [Doctoral Dissertation, Arizona State University]. Arts Education Partnership. (2011). *Music matters: How music education helps students learn, achieve, and succeed.* https://www.aep-arts.org/wp-content/uploads/Music-Matters-1.pdf

PART I

1. Angelou, M. (2008). *Letter to my daughter.* Random House.

CHAPTER 1

1. Oxford English Dictionary. (2023). Love. In *Oxford English dictionary.* https://www.oed.com/view dictionaryentry/Entry/110566
2. Boyatzis, R. E., Rochford, K., & Taylor, S. N. (2015). The role of the positive emotional attractor in vision and shared vision: Toward effective leadership, relationships, and engagement. *Frontiers in Psychology, 6,* 1–13.
3. Cotter-Lockard, D. (2012). *Chamber music coaching strategies and rehearsal techniques that enable collaboration* [Doctoral Dissertation, Fielding Graduate University], p. 182.
4. Edmondson, A. (1999). Psychological safety and learning behavior in work teams. *Administrative Science Quarterly, 44*(2), 350–383.
5. Teachout, T. (2012, August 30). Why comedy is truer to life than tragedy. *The Wall Street Journal.*

CHAPTER 2

1. Boyatzis, R. E., Passarelli, A. M., Koenig, K., Lowe, M., Mathew, B., Stoller, J. K., & Phillips, M. (2012). Examination of the neural substrates activated in memories of experiences with resonant and dissonant leaders. *The Leadership Quarterly, 23*(2), 259–272.
2. Steinhardt, A. (2000). *Indivisible by four,* p. 242. Farrar, Straus and Giroux.
3. Covey, S. (2020). *The 7 habits of highly effective people.* Simon & Schuster.
4. Harvard University. (2023). *Program on negotiation.* https://www.pon.harvard.edu/
5. Dictionary.com. (2023). Kvetch. In *Dictionary.com.* https://www.dictionary.com/browse/kvetch
6. Boyatzis, R. E., Passarelli, A. M., Koenig, K., Lowe, M., Mathew, B., Stoller, J. K., & Phillips, M. (2012). Examination of the neural substrates activated in memories of experiences with resonant and dissonant leaders. *The Leadership Quarterly, 23*(2), 259–272.
7. Ruiz, M. (1997). *The four agreements: A practical guide to personal freedom.* Amber-Allen Publishers.

192　Notes

8. Brandt, N. (1993). *Con brio: Four Russians called the Budapest String Quartet*, p. 50. Oxford University Press.
9. Alger, D. (n.d.). *Rules of improv.* Pan Theater. https://www.pantheater.com/rules-of-improv.html
10. Fey, T. (2011). *Bossypants*, pp. 84–85. Little, Brown and Company.
11. Brandt, N. (1993). *Con Brio: Four Russians called the Budapest String Quartet*, pp. 127–128. Authors Choice Press.
12. Frager, R., & Fadiman, J. (2005). *Personality and personal growth* (6th ed.). Pearson Prentice Hall.
13. Kumar, U. (2016). *The Wiley handbook of personality assessment*. John Wiley & Sons, Inc.
14. Goleman, D. (2006). *Emotional intelligence* (10th anniversary ed.). Bantam Books.
15. Boyatzis, R. E., Passarelli, A. M., Koenig, K., Lowe, M., Mathew, B., Stoller, J. K., & Phillips, M. (2012). Examination of the neural substrates activated in memories of experiences with resonant and dissonant leaders. *The Leadership Quarterly*, 23(2), 259–272.
16. Goleman, D. (2006). *Emotional intelligence* (10th anniversary ed.). Bantam Books.
17. Goleman, D., Boyatzis, R. E., & McKee, A. (2002). *Primal leadership: Realizing the power of emotional intelligence*. Harvard Business School Press.
18. Bradberry, T., & Greaves, J. (2009). *Emotional intelligence 2.0*. TalentSmart.

CHAPTER 3

1. Perlman, I. (2010, June 28). *Itzhak on practicing* [Video]. YouTube. https://youtu.be/h3xEHigWShM
2. Klickstein, G. (2009). *The musician's way: A guide to practice, performances, and wellness*. Oxford University Press.
3. Encyclopedia Britannica. (n.d.). Drone. In *Encyclopedia Britannica*. https://www.britannica.com/art/drone-music
4. Kolisch, R. (1993). Tempo and character in Beethoven's music. *The Musical Quarterly*, 77(1), 90–131. Kolisch, R. (1993). Tempo and character in Beethoven's music. *The Musical Quarterly*, 77(2), 268–342.

CHAPTER 4

1. Vaartstra, B. (2018, March 26). *Using motivic development to create musical themes* [Podcast and Blog]. Learn Jazz Standards. https://www.learnjazzstandards.com/ljs-podcast/play-better-jazz-solos/ljs-108-using-motivic-development-to-create-musical-themes/
2. Kolisch, R. (1993). Tempo and character in Beethoven's music. *The Musical Quarterly*, 77(1), 90–131. Kolisch, R. (1993). Tempo and character in Beethoven's music. *The Musical Quarterly*, 77(2), 268–342.
3. Oxford Dictionary of Music (2023). Dynamics. In *Oxford dictionary of music*. https://www.oxfordlearnersdictionaries.com/
4. Hewitt, M. (2013). *Musical scales of the world*. The Note Tree.
5. Descartes, R. (1997). The passions of the soul (Elizabeth S. Haldane & G. R. T. Ross, Trans.). In E. Chávez-Arvizo (Ed.), *Key philosophical writings* (pp. 358–383). Wordsworth Editions Limited. (Original work published 1649). Hall, S. K. (2017). The doctrine of affections: Where art meets reason. *Musical Offerings*, 8(2), Article 2, 51–64.
6. Wright, F. L. (2005). *Frank Lloyd Wright: An autobiography*. Pomegranate.
7. Titon, J. (2016). *Worlds of music: An introduction to the music of the world's peoples*. Cengage Learning EMEA.
8. Grove Dictionary of Music and Musicians. (2004). Sonata form. In *Grove dictionary of music and musicians*. https://doi.org/10.1093/gmo/9781561592630.article.26197

Notes **193**

9. Benward, B., & Saker, M. (2009). *Music in theory and practice* (Vol. 2), p. 266. McGraw-Hill.
10. Heifetz International Music Institute. (2018, January 9). *Debussy: String quartet in G minor—Borromeo Quartet* [Video]. YouTube. https://youtu.be/HLag9JE2ihY

CHAPTER 5

1. Isacoff, S. (2003). *Temperament: How music became a battleground for the great minds of western civilization*. Vintage Books.
2. Duffin, R. (2007). *How equal temperament ruined harmony (and why you should care)*. W. W. Norton & Co.

CHAPTER 6

1. Higham, T., Basell, L., Jacobic, R., Wood, R., Ramsey, C. B., & Conard, M. J. (2012). Testing models for the beginnings of the Aurignacian and the advent of figurative art and music: The radiocarbon chronology of Geißenklösterle. *Journal of Human Evolution, 62*(6), 664–676.
2. de Botton, A., & Armstrong, J. (2016). *Art as therapy*, p. 56. Phaidon Press Limited.
3. Irvine, J., Kashkashian, K., LaCourse, M., Ramsey, L., Ritscher, K., & Rodland, C. (2020). *The Karen Tuttle legacy: A resource and guide for viola students, teachers, and performers*. Carl Fischer Publishers.
4. This list was provided to us by Nicholas Kitchen, first violin, Borromeo Quartet. He heard about the list from a lecture given by pianist Thomas Sauer. The list was derived from Czerny, Carl. (1970). *On the proper performance of all Beethoven's works for the piano*, (Paul Badura-Skoda, Ed. & Trans.), U.S. Edition, T. Presser, Universal Edition.
5. Sacks, O. (2008). *Musicophilia*. Vintage Books.
6. Sacks, O. (2008). *Musicophilia*, p. 180. Vintage Books.
7. Smetana, B. (1991). *Quartetto I. Mi minore. Z mého života* [Musical score]. Editio Supraphon.
8. Okantah, M. S. (2004). *Reconnecting memories: Dreams no longer deferred*. Africa World Press.
9. Peckham, M. (2004). *Breakfast at the Ibis*. Unpublished work.
10. Lieberman, J. L. (1998). *Planet musician: The world music sourcebook for musicians*. Hal Leonard Corporation.
11. World Music Network. (2023). *Rough guides*. https://worldmusic.net/collections/rough-guides

CHAPTER 7

1. Scott, D. (2017, November 2). *How Claude Monet documented light using the Rouen Cathedral*. Draw Paint Academy. https://drawpaintacademy.com/claude-monet-rouen-cathedral
2. Bartók, B., Jr. (1976). Remembering my father, Béla Bartók. In T. Crow (Ed.), *Bartók studies* (pp. 149–151). Information Coordinators.
3. Curcio, A. K. (2009). A tribute to nature: The evolution of the night-music style in Bartók's music. *Nota Bene: Canadian Undergraduate Journal of Musicology, 2*(1), Article 5, 63–71.
4. Burleigh, H. T. (1918). *Sometimes I feel like a motherless child*. Historic Sheet Music Collection. https://digitalcommons.conncoll.edu/sheetmusic/1283
5. Cooper, B., Coldicott, A. L., Drabkin, W., & Marston, N. (1991). *The Beethoven compendium: A guide to Beethoven's life and music* (pp. 169–170). Thames & Hudson Ltd.
6. Barrett, C. E. (2006). What every musician needs to know about the body: Plan for incorporating body mapping in music instruction. *American String Teacher, 56*(4), 34–37.

194   Notes

CHAPTER 8

1. Huygens, C., & Nijhoff, M. (1893, 1932). *Oeuvres complètes de Christiaan Huygens* (Vols. 5, 17). La Société Hollandaise Des Sciences.
2. King, E. C., & Ginsborg, J. (2011). Gestures and glances: Interactions in ensemble rehearsal. In A. Gritten & E. C. King (Eds.), *New perspectives on music and gesture* (pp. 177–202). Ashgate. Clayton, M., Sager, R., & Will, U. (2005). In time with the music: The concept of entrainment and its significance for ethnomusicology. *European Meetings in Ethnomusicology 11*(1), 1–82.
3. Yeap, R. (2021, March 7). *Leonard Bernstein conducting Haydn Symphony No. 88, using his face* [Video]. YouTube. https://youtu.be/4WvTQb4MonI

CHAPTER 9

1. Davidson, J., & Correia, J. S. (2002). Body movement. In R. Parncutt & G. McPherson (Eds.), *The science and psychology of music performance: Creative strategies for teaching and learning*, pp. 237–250. Oxford University Press. King, E. C., & Ginsborg, J. (2011). Gestures and glances: Interactions in ensemble rehearsal. In A. Gritten & E. C. King (Eds.), *New perspectives on music and gesture*, pp. 177–202. Ashgate. Davidson, J. W. (2012). Bodily movement and facial actions in expressive musical performance by solo and duo instrumentalists: Two distinctive case studies. *Psychology of Music, 40*(5), 595–633.
2. BAPNE Method (*Biomecánica. Anatomía. Psicología. Neurociencia. Etnomusicología*: Biomechanics, Anatomy, Psychology, Neuroscience, Ethnomusicology, see https://percusion-corporal. com) was created by Javier Romero Naranjo, who describes it as "a method of cognitive, socioemotional, psychomotor and neurorehabilitative stimulation based on neuromotor skills. It uses body percussion as a didactic resource focused on the possible stimulation of cognitive and executive functions." We first learned about the BAPNE Method from Adriana Linares, violist of the Dalí String Quartet.

   Dalcroze eurhythmics is a process for awakening, developing, and refining innate musicality through rhythmic movement, ear training, and improvisation (https://dalcrozeusa.org).
3. Levin, T. Y. (1993). Integral interpretation: Introductory notes to Beethoven, Kolisch, and the question of the metronome. *Musical Quarterly, 77*(1), 81–89.
4. Kolisch, R. (1943). Tempo and character in Beethoven's music. *Musical Quarterly, 29*, 169–187, 292–312.
5. Kennedy, M., & Kennedy, J. (2013). *The Oxford dictionary of music.* Oxford Quick Reference.
6. Hoppin, R. H. (1978). *Medieval music*, p. 221. W. W. Norton.
7. Kahn, A. E. (1970). *Joys and sorrows: Reflections by Pablo Casals.* Simon & Schuster.
8. White, J. D. (1976). *The analysis of music.* Prentice-Hall.
9. Reed, T. (1997). *Progressive steps to syncopation for the modern drummer*, p. 33. Alfred Music Publishing.
10. Per email conversation with Donald Weilerstein, August 21, 2023.
11. Hartenberger, R., & McClelland, R. (Eds.). (2020). *The Cambridge companion to rhythm.* Cambridge University Press.
12. Oxford Reference. (2023). Agogic. In *Oxford reference.* https://www.oxfordreference.com/view/ 10.1093/oi/authority.20110803095356331
13. Mostovoy, M., & Lehrer, C. D. (2023). *Marcel Tabuteau first-hand: In Tabuteau's own words.* https:// marceltabuteau.com/tabuteau-system/marc-mostovoy/in-tabuteaus-own-words/

Notes   195

CHAPTER 10

1. Isacoff, S. (2003). *Temperament: How music became a battleground for the great minds of western civilization*. Vintage Books.
2. Duffin, R. (2007). *How equal temperament ruined harmony (and why you should care)*. W. W. Norton & Co.
3. CelloBello. (2017). *Paul Katz*. https://www.cellobello.org/cello-blog/author/paul-katz
4. Isacoff, S. (2003). *Temperament: How music became a battleground for the great minds of western civilization*. Vintage Books. Duffin, R. (2007). *How equal temperament ruined harmony (and why you should care)*. W. W. Norton & Co.
5. Jensen, H. J., & Chung, M. R. (2017). *CelloMind: Intonation and technique*. Ovation Press.
6. Jensen, H. J., Chung, M. R., & Kalinovsky, G. (2019). *ViolinMind: Intonation and technique*. Ovation Press.
7. Sessions, R. (1951). *Harmonic practice*, pp. 3, 11. Harcourt & Brace.
8. Hindemith, P. (1979). *Elementary training for musicians*. Schott Publishing.
9. Laitz, S. G. (2016). *The complete musician: An integrated approach to theory, analysis, and listening* (4th ed.). Oxford University Press.
10. Lieberman, J. L. (1998). *Planet musician: The world music sourcebook for musicians*. Hal Leonard Corporation.
11. Sturman, J. (Ed.). (2019). *The SAGE international encyclopedia of music and culture* (Vol. 1), pp. 2167–2170. SAGE Publications.
12. Czajkowski, A. M. L., Greasley, A. E., & Allis, M. (2022). Mindfulness for musicians: A mixed methods study investigating the effects of 8-week mindfulness courses on music students at a leading conservatoire. *Musicae Scientiae, 26*(2), 259–279.

CHAPTER 11

1. Fairfield County Children's Choir. (n.d.). *Vocal and choral techniques*. https://www.singfccc.org/wp-content/uploads/Vocal-Choral-Techniques-Fairfield-U.pdf
2. Nam, K. (2014). *Introduction of musical rhetoric*. https://keehun.com/writings/introduction-to-the-introduction-of-musical-rhetoric/
3. Merriam Webster. (2023). Sforzando. In *Merriam Webster dictionary*. https://www.merriam-webster.com/dictionary/sforzando
4. Mozart, L. (1756, 1985). *A treatise on the fundamentals of violin playing* (A. Einstein & E. Knocker, Trans.). Oxford University Press.

CHAPTER 12

1. Antiwar Songs. (2009, June 30). *Sometimes I feel like a motherless child*. https://www.antiwarsongs.org/canzone.php?id=10617&lang=en
2. The Music Settlement. (2021, February 18). Cavani Quartet performs "Midnight Child" [Video]. YouTube. https://youtu.be/yAf4LdfaY1Y
3. Burrows, G. (2018, October 29). How scat singing became an expressive language in its own right. *The Independent*. https://www.independent.co.uk/arts-entertainment/music/features/scat-singing-definition-jazz-history-louis-armstrong-ella-fitzgerald-cab-calloway-slavery-african-americans-a8607061.html

196 Notes

4. SearchUSAPeople. (2013, December 17). *Ella Fitzgerald the master of scat singing* [Video]. YouTube. https://youtu.be/nrcIsUH6RfI
5. Murakami, H., & Ozawa, S. (2016). *Absolutely on music: Conversations with Seiji Ozawa* (J. Rubin, Trans.), p. 302. Harvill Secker.

CHAPTER 13

1. Mendelssohn, F. (1825). *Octet in E-flat Major, Op. 20.*
2. Cotter-Lockard, D. (2012). *Chamber music coaching strategies and rehearsal techniques that enable collaboration* [Doctoral Dissertation, Fielding Graduate University], p. 182.

CHAPTER 14

1. Spolin Games Online. (2018). *Improv games.* https://spolingamesonline.org/games/improv-games/mirror-games/
2. Overy, K., & Molnar-Szakacs, I. (2009). Being together in time: Musical experience and the mirror neuron system. *Music Perception, 26*(5), 489–504.
3. Clayton, M., Sager, R., & Will, U. (2005). In time with the music: The concept of entrainment and its significance for ethnomusicology. *European Meetings in Ethnomusicology, 11*(1), 1–82. Phillips-Silver, J., Aktipis, C. A., & Bryant, G. A. (2010). The ecology of entrainment: Foundations of coordinated rhythmic movement. *Music Perception, 28*(1), 3–14.
4. Laughter for a Change. (2013, May 30). *The mirror game* [Video]. YouTube. https://youtu.be/JTEjiJfJkNU
5. Barnaveokprueba. (2012, October 11). *Lucille Ball and Harpo Marx the mirror routine* [Video]. YouTube. https://youtu.be/79EnDc-Ucv8
6. Cotter-Lockard, D. (2012). *Chamber music coaching strategies and rehearsal techniques that enable collaboration* [Doctoral Dissertation, Fielding Graduate University].

Appendix D

1. Niles, L. (2012, December 15). *The Violinist.com glossary of violin-related terms.* Violinist.com. https://www.violinist.com/blog/laurie/201212/14226/
2. Fischer, S. (2022). *Basics: 300 exercises and practice routines for the violin.* Alfred Music.

Bibliography

Alger, D. (n.d.). *Rules of improv*. Pan Theater. https://www.pantheater.com/rules-of-improv.html

Angelou, M. (2008). *Letter to my daughter*. Random House.

Antiwar Songs. (2009, June 30). *Sometimes I feel like a motherless child*. https://www.antiwarsongs.org/canzone.php?id=10617&lang=en

Arts Education Partnership. (2011). *Music matters: How music education helps students learn, achieve, and succeed*. https://www.aep-arts.org/wp-content/uploads/Music-Matters-1.pdf.

Barnaveokprueba. (2012, October 11). *Lucille Ball and Harpo Marx the mirror routine* [Video]. YouTube. https://youtu.be/79EnDc-Ucv8.

Barrett, C. E. (2006). What every musician needs to know about the body: Plan for incorporating body mapping in music instruction. *American String Teacher, 56*(4), 34–37.

Bartók, B., Jr. (1976). Remembering my father, Béla Bartók. In T. Crow (Ed.), *Bartók studies* (pp. 149–151). Information Coordinators.

Benward, B., & Saker, M. (2009). *Music in theory and practice* (Vol. 2). McGraw-Hill.

Boyatzis, R. E., Passarelli, A. M., Koenig, K., Lowe, M., Mathew, B., Stoller, J. K., & Phillips, M. (2012). Examination of the neural substrates activated in memories of experiences with resonant and dissonant leaders. *The Leadership Quarterly, 23*(2), 259–272.

Boyatzis, R. E., Rochford, K., & Taylor, S. N. (2015). The role of the positive emotional attractor in vision and shared vision: Toward effective leadership, relationships, and engagement. *Frontiers in Psychology, 6*, 1–13.

Bradberry, T., & Greaves, J. (2009). *Emotional intelligence 2.0*. TalentSmart.

Brandt, N. (1993). *Con brio: Four Russians called the Budapest String Quartet*. Oxford University Press.

Burleigh, H. T. (1918). *Sometimes I feel like a motherless child*. Historic Sheet Music Collection. https://digitalcommons.conncoll.edu/sheetmusic/1283

Burrows, G. (2018, October 29). How scat singing became an expressive language in its own right. *The Independent*. https://www.independent.co.uk/arts-entertainment/music/features/scat-singing-definition-jazz-history-louis-armstrong-ella-fitzgerald-cab-calloway-slavery-african-americans-a8607061.html

CelloBello. (2017). *Paul Katz*. https://www.cellobello.org/cello-blog/author/paul-katz

Clayton, M., Sager, R., & Will, U. (2005). In time with the music: The concept of entrainment and its significance for ethnomusicology. *European Meetings in Ethnomusicology, 11*(1), 1–82.

Cooper, B., Coldicott, A. L., Drabkin, W., & Marston, N. (1991). *The Beethoven compendium: A guide to Beethoven's life and music*. Thames & Hudson Ltd.

Cotter-Lockard, D. (2012). *Chamber music coaching strategies and rehearsal techniques that enable collaboration* [Doctoral Dissertation, Fielding Graduate University].

Covey, S. (2020). *The 7 habits of highly effective people*. Simon & Schuster.

Curcio, A. K. (2009). A tribute to nature: The evolution of the night-music style in Bartók's music. *Nota Bene: Canadian Undergraduate Journal of Musicology, 2*(1), Article 5, 63–71.

Czajkowski, A. M. L., Greasley, A. E., & Allis, M. (2022). Mindfulness for musicians: A mixed methods study investigating the effects of 8-week mindfulness courses on music students at a leading conservatoire. *Musicae Scientiae, 26*(2), 259–279.

Davidson, J. W. (2012). Bodily movement and facial actions in expressive musical performance by solo and duo instrumentalists: Two distinctive case studies. *Psychology of Music, 40*(5), 595–633.

Davidson, J. W., & Correia, J. S. (2002). Body movement. In R. Parncutt & G. McPherson (Eds.), *The science and psychology of music performance: Creative strategies for teaching and learning* (pp. 237–250). Oxford University Press.

Descartes, R. (1997). The passions of the soul (Elizabeth S. Haldane & G. R. T. Ross, Trans.). In E. Chávez-Arvizo (Ed.), *Key philosophical writings* (pp. 358–383). Wordsworth Editions Limited. (Original work published 1649)

de Botton, A., & Armstrong, J. (2016). *Art as therapy*. Phaidon Press Limited.

Dictionary.com. (2023). Kvetch. In *Dictionary.com*. https://www.dictionary.com/browse/kvetch

198 Bibliography

Duffin, R. (2007). *How equal temperament ruined harmony (and why you should care)*. W. W. Norton & Co.

Edmondson, A. (1999). Psychological safety and learning behavior in work teams. *Administrative Science Quarterly, 44*(2), 350–383.

Encyclopedia Britannica. (n.d.). Drone. In *Encyclopedia Britannica*. https://www.britannica.com/art/drone-music

Fairfield County Children's Choir. (n.d.). *Vocal and choral techniques*. https://www.singfccc.org/wp-content/uploads/Vocal-Choral-Techniques-Fairfield-U.pdf

Fey, T. (2011). *Bossypants*. Little, Brown and Company.

Fischer, S. (2022). *Basics: 300 exercises and practice routines for the violin*. Alfred Music.

Frager, R., & Fadiman, J. (2005). *Personality and personal growth* (6th ed.). Pearson Prentice Hall.

Goleman, D. (2006). *Emotional intelligence* (10th anniversary ed.). Bantam Books.

Goleman, D., Boyatzis, R. E., & McKee, A. (2002). *Primal leadership: Realizing the power of emotional intelligence*. Harvard Business School Press.

Grove Dictionary of Music and Musicians. (2004). Sonata form. In *Grove Dictionary of Music and Musicians*. https://doi.org/10.1093/gmo/9781561592630.article.26197

Hall, S. K. (2017). The doctrine of affections: Where art meets reason. *Musical Offerings, 8*(2), Article 2, 51–64.

Hartenberger, R., & McClelland, R. (Eds.). (2020). *The Cambridge companion to rhythm*. Cambridge University Press.

Harvard University. (2023). *Program on negotiation*. https://www.pon.harvard.edu/

Heifetz International Music Institute. (2018, January 9). *Debussy: String Quartet in G Minor—Borromeo Quartet* [Video]. YouTube. https://youtu.be/HLag9JE2ihY

Hewitt, M. (2013). *Musical scales of the world*. The Note Tree.

Higham, T., Basell, L., Jacobic, R., Wood, R., Ramsey, C. B., & Conard, M. J. (2012). Testing models for the beginnings of the Aurignacian and the advent of figurative art and music: The radiocarbon chronology of Geißenklösterle. *Journal of Human Evolution, 62*(6), 664–676.

Hindemith, P. (1979). *Elementary training for musicians*. Schott Publishing.

Hoppin, R. H. (1978). *Medieval music*. W. W. Norton.

Huygens, C., & Nijhoff, M. (1893, 1932). *Oeuvres complètes de Christiaan Huygens* (Vols. 5, 17). La Société Hollandaise Des Sciences.

Irvine, J., Kashkashian, K., LaCourse, M., Ramsey, L., Ritscher, K., & Rodland, C. (2020). *The Karen Tuttle legacy: A resource and guide for viola students, teachers, and performers*. Carl Fischer Publishers.

Isacoff, S. (2003). *Temperament: How music became a battleground for the great minds of western civilization*. Vintage Books.

Jensen, H. J., & Chung, M. R. (2017). *CelloMind: Intonation and technique*. Ovation Press, Ltd.

Jensen, H. J., Chung, M. R., & Kalinovsky, G. (2019). *ViolinMind: Intonation and technique*. Ovation Press, Ltd.

Kahn, A. E. (1970). *Joys and Sorrows: Reflections by Pablo Casals*. Simon & Schuster.

Kennedy, M., & Kennedy, J. (2013). *The Oxford dictionary of music*. Oxford Quick Reference. https://www.oxfordreference.com/display/10.1093/oi/authority.20110803100153475#:~:text=Term%20used%20of%20regular%20succession,as%20different%20kinds%20of%20metres.

King, E. C., & Ginsborg, J. (2011). Gestures and glances: Interactions in ensemble rehearsal. In A. Gritten & E. C. King (Eds.), *New perspectives on music and gesture* (pp. 177–202). Ashgate.

Klickstein, G. (2009). *The musician's way: A guide to practice, performances, and wellness*. Oxford University Press.

Kokotsaki, D., & Hallam, S. (2007). Higher education music students' perceptions of the benefits of participative music making. *Music Education Research, 9*(1), 93–109.

Kolisch, R. (1993). Tempo and character in Beethoven's music. *The Musical Quarterly, 77*(1), 90–131.

Kolisch, R. (1993). Tempo and character in Beethoven's music. *The Musical Quarterly, 77*(2), 268–342.

Kumar, U. (2016). *The Wiley handbook of personality assessment*. John Wiley & Sons, Inc.

Laitz, S. G. (2016). *The complete musician: An integrated approach to theory, analysis, and listening* (4th ed.). Oxford University Press.

Bibliography 199

Larson, D. D. (2010). *The effects of chamber music experience on music performance achievement, motivation, and attitudes among high school band students* [Doctoral dissertation, Arizona State University].

Laughter for a Change. (2013, May 30). *The mirror game* [Video]. YouTube. https://youtu.be/JTEjiJfJkNU

Levin, T. Y. (1993). Integral interpretation: Introductory notes to Beethoven, Kolisch, and the question of the metronome. *Musical Quarterly, 77*(1), 81–89.

Lieberman, J. L. (1998). *Planet musician: The world music sourcebook for musicians.* Hal Leonard Corporation.

Mendelssohn, F. (1825). *Octet in E-flat Major, Op. 20.*

Merriam Webster. (2023). Sforzando. In *Merriam Webster dictionary.* https://www.merriam-webster.com/dictionary/sforzando

Mostovoy, M., & Lehrer, C. D. (2023). *Marcel Tabuteau first-hand: In Tabuteau's own words.* https://marceltabuteau.com/tabuteau-system/marc-mostovoy/in-tabuteaus-own-words/

Mozart, L. (1756, 1985). *A treatise on the fundamentals of violin playing* (A. Einstein & E. Knocker, Trans). Oxford University Press.

Murakami, H., & Ozawa, S. (2016). *Absolutely on music: Conversations with Seiji Ozawa* (J. Rubin, Trans.). Harvill Secker.

The Music Settlement. (2021, February 18). Cavani Quartet performs "Midnight Child" [Video]. YouTube. https://youtu.be/yAf4LdfaY1Y

Nam, K. (2014). *Introduction of musical rhetoric.* https://keehun.com/writings/introduction-to-the-introduction-of-musical-rhetoric/

Niles, L. (2012, December 15). *The Violinist.com glossary of violin-related terms.* Violinist.com. https://www.violinist.com/blog/laurie/201212/14226/

Okantah, M. S. (2004). *Reconnecting memories: Dreams no longer deferred.* Africa World Press.

Overy, K., & Molnar-Szakacs, I. (2009). Being together in time: Musical experience and the mirror neuron system. *Music Perception, 26*(5), 489–504.

Oxford Dictionary of Music. (2023). Dynamics. In *Oxford Dictionary of Music.* https://www.oxfordlearnersdictionaries.com/

Oxford English Dictionary. (2023). Love. In *Oxford English dictionary.* https://www.oed.com/viewdictionaryentry/Entry/110566

Oxford Reference. (2023). Agogic. In *Oxford reference.* https://www.oxfordreference.com/view/10.1093/oi/authority.20110803095356331

Peckham, M. (2004). *Breakfast at the Ibis.* Unpublished work.

Perlman, I. (2010, June 28). *Itzhak on practicing* [Video]. YouTube. https://youtu.be/h3xEHigWShM

Phillips-Silver, J., Aktipis, C. A., & Bryant, G. A. (2010). The ecology of entrainment: Foundations of coordinated rhythmic movement. *Music Perception, 28*(1), 3–14.

Reed, T. (1997). *Progressive steps to syncopation for the modern drummer.* Alfred Music Publishing.

Ruiz, M. (1997). *The four agreements: A practical guide to personal freedom.* Amber-Allen Publishers.

Sacks, O. (2008). *Musicophilia.* Vintage Books.

Scott, D. (2017, November 2). *How Claude Monet documented light using the Rouen Cathedral.* Draw Paint Academy. https://drawpaintacademy.com/claude-monet-rouen-cathedral

SearchUSAPeople. (2013, December 17). *Ella Fitzgerald the master of scat singing* [Video]. YouTube. https://youtu.be/nrcIsUH6RfI

Sessions, R. (1951). *Harmonic practice.* Harcourt & Brace.

Smetana, B. (1991). *Quartetto I. Mi minore. Z mého života* [Musical score]. Editio Supraphon.

Spolin Games Online. (2018). *Improv games.* https://spolingamesonline.org/games/improv-games/mirror-games/

Steinhardt, A. (2000). *Indivisible by four.* Farrar, Straus and Giroux.

Sturman, J. (Ed.). (2019). Musical Texture. In *The SAGE international encyclopedia of music and culture* (Vol. 1, pp. 2167–2170). SAGE Publications, Inc.

Teachout, T. (2012, August 30). Why comedy is truer to life than tragedy. *The Wall Street Journal.*

Titon, J. (2016). *Worlds of music: An introduction to the music of the world's peoples.* Cengage Learning EMEA.

200 Bibliography

Vaartstra, B. (2018, March 26). *Using motivic development to create musical themes* [Podcast and Blog]. Learn Jazz Standards. https://www.learnjazzstandards.com/ljs-podcast/play-better-jazz-solos/ljs-108-using-motivic-development-to-create-musical-themes/

White, J. D. (1976). *The analysis of music*. Prentice-Hall.

Wright, F. L. (2005). *Frank Lloyd Wright: An autobiography*. Pomegranate.

World Music Network. (2023). *Rough guides*. https://worldmusic.net/collections/rough-guides

Yeap, R. (2021, March 7). *Leonard Bernstein conducting Haydn Symphony No. 88, using his face* [Video]. YouTube. https://youtu.be/4WvTQb4MonI